To Tom Heller,

With compliments of the author.

Ham Leung Sto
22 October 2007
New York

Asia-Pacific Leadership Series

BEYOND THE SHADOW OF 9/11

A YEAR AT THE UNITED NATIONS
GENERAL ASSEMBLY

Han Seung-soo
President
The 56th Session of the United
Nations General Assembly

THE EDWIN O.
REISCHAUER CENTER
FOR EAST ASIAN STUDIES
WASHINGTON D.C.

The Paul H. Nitze School of Advanced International Studies
Johns Hopkins University

The Edwin O. Reischauer Center for East Asian Studies
Established in 1984, with the explicit support of the Reischauer family, the Edwin O. Reischauer Center for East Asian Studies at the Paul H. Nitze School of Advanced International Studies (SAIS) actively supports the research and study of trans-Pacific and intra-Asian relations to advance mutual understanding between North-east Asia and the United States.

The first Japanese-born and Japanese-speaking U.S. Ambassador to Japan, Edwin O. Reischauer (serv. 1961-66) later served as the center's Honorary Chair from its founding until 1990. His wife Haru Matsukata Reischauer followed as Honorary Chair from 1991 to 1998. They both exemplified the deep commitment that the Reischauer Center aspires to perpetuate in its scholarly and cultural activities today.

Asia-Pacific Leadership Series, No. 1
Published by The Edwin O. Reischauer Center for East Asian Studies, Johns Hopkins University–SAIS
1619 Massachusetts Avenue, NW
Washington, D.C. 20036
Tel. 202.663.5812   Fax: 202.663.5891
©2007 by Han Seung-Soo
All rights reserved
Printed in the USA
Cover design by Automated Graphics Systems, Inc., White Plains, MD
ISBN-13: 978-0-9797093-0-2
ISBN-10: 0-9797093-0-X

For Soja

Wife and Best Friend

Contents

viii

Foreword

Kent E. Calder
Director, Reischauer Center for East Asian Studies

The Reischauer Center for East Asian Studies is honored to publish this extraordinary, first-person record of tragedy and triumph at the United Nations in the shadow of "9/11." Dr. Han Seung-soo has a distinguished record as one of Asia's most notable global statesmen, having served not only as President of the UN General Assembly over the fateful year that is chronicled here, but also as Korean Foreign Minister, Minister of Trade and Industry, Minister of Finance, Chief of Staff to the Korean President, Deputy Prime Minister, and Ambassador to the United States. Han is also a trenchant, sometimes poetic writer, formerly a professor at Korea's distinguished Seoul National University, who vividly retells momentous events and gives us an unusual inside view of how the world's principal global peacekeeping body actually operates in time of crisis.

This volume, covering Dr. Han Seung-soo's activities as President of the UN General Assembly from September 2001 until September 2002, stands out as a historical record for two major reasons. It gives us, first of all, an unusual personal view from the top of watershed events: the UN's response to 9/11 and the problem of global terrorism; the invasion of Afghanistan; the first World Economic Forum held outside Davos; and the Nobel Committee's decision to award its prestigious Peace Prize to the United Nations. Dr. Han's first-person account of receiving the Prize in Oslo, together with Secretary-General Kofi Annan, and participating as a principal in the related festivities is a major highlight of the book.

At the same time it chronicles momentous events, this volume also contains insights into the personal histories of distinguished individuals who have shaped our times: not only Dr. Han but also "America's Mayor," Rudy Giuliani, who gave a historic, first-ever New York mayor's UN address during Dr. Han's tenure; President George W. Bush, who also made his first-ever visit to the United

Nations to speak under Dr. Han's dias; and Secretary of State Colin Powell, with whom Dr. Han held a historic foreign-ministers' meeting immediately after the 9/11 attacks. The recently inaugurated Secretary-General of the United Nations, Ban Ki-moon, crosses these pages in particular detail, beginning with the dramatic moment when Ban handed his mentor a hastily scrawled note describing the World Trade Center attack that had occurred only minutes before, amidst the preparatory ceremonies attending Han's inauguration as UN President that very day. Ban, a confidante of many years, was serving as Han's Chef de Cabinet and was thus the only person able to convey such sensitive and momentous information.

Apart from the chronicle of fateful events and prominent personalities that have shaped our times that this book provides, this memoir also yields insights into Korea's unique relationship with the United Nations. As Dr. Han points out, the Republic of Korea (ROK) has only been a member of the UN since 1991. Yet it is one of the few nations that celebrates United Nations Day as an official holiday and the only advanced industrial nation with UN troops still stationed on its soil. Koreans even have a commonly known "Song of the United Nations."

Apart from Dr. Han's presidency at the General Assembly, although in many cases inspired by it, the ROK has played an extraordinary recent role in UN leadership. Former Foreign Minister Han Seung-joo served, for example, as the Secretary-General's Representative for Cyprus (1996–97) and as a member of the UN Inquiry Commission on the 1994 Rwandan Genocide (1999); Lee Jong-wook as director of the World Health Organization (2003–06); and Hahm Chaibong as Director of the UNESCO Division of Social Science Research and Policy (2003–05), before the elevation of former Foreign Minister Ban Ki-moon at the beginning of 2007 to his current standing as UN Secretary-General. South Korea has also played a major recent role in UN peacekeeping, deploying troops to seven countries since 1993 and election monitors to another five.

This book helps explain this distinctive Korean commitment to UN activities, which could well have broader implications for further strengthening the world body.

As Dr. Han himself notes, "From childhood, the United Nations had been the embodiment of my hopes and dreams. Although Korea had won independence from Japan in 1945, the nation then had to suffer the tragedy of being divided into South and North. The people of the two Koreas, sharing a common national and cultural heritage, yet separated by ideology, fought in the Korean War (1950–53). While enduring this tragedy, the only source of hope for the citizens of South Korea was the United Nations."

In reality, as Dr. Han points out, UN support for Korea's peaceful, democratic evolution predates even the Korean War. It was the UN Temporary Commission on Korea (UNTCOK), founded in late 1947, that supervised the democratic election of Korea's first National Assembly and the formal establishment of the Republic of Korea on August 15, 1948. It was the UN General Assembly that legitimated the fledgling Rhee administration as the only legitimate government on the Korean Peninsula, and UN resolutions that provided the basis for 16 nations, including the United States, to enter the Korean War and fight for three years side by side with South Korean forces. After the war, the UN continued to support Korean economic growth and development through the United Nations Korean Reconstruction Agency (UNKRA).

The United Nations has thus played a central role in Korea's transition to prosperity and democracy, which Koreans appear to fully appreciate. With a Korean now serving as Secretary-General, and with seasoned advisors such as Dr. Han in support, the political stage would thus appear to be set for a proactive Korean role both on issues of global development and of international peacekeeping. Should the Korean Peninsula itself move toward unification, a partnership between the United Nations and Korea to ease the complex challenges of transition through broad cooperation with the world community would be firmly in place.

This book provides us with a fascinating inside look at the awesome challenges that running a truly global organization of close to 200 Member States actually involves. We get a chance to see up close the sheer complexity, the inevitable staff tensions, and the shifting regional coalitions that prevail at the United Nations. After reading this book, it is much easier to see how the UN can be so cosmopolitan in its outlook and at times also so rigid on matters of major international import, such as the reform of the Security Council. Dr. Han, the record shows, remained scrupulously neutral, as the General Assembly President. Yet, his description of the complex struggle among "aspirants," "pretenders," and a "Coffee Club" of around 30 nations hesitant about Security Council expansion helps us understand why more than a decade of continuous efforts to reform the Council, with the support of the United States, Germany, Japan, India, and several other major powers, has yet to produce substantive results.

In the end, the most important contributions of this book, of course, are the insights that it gives us into the remarkable career of its author. At one level, it is the classic story of a fantastic dream— by a young boy in a small Korean town who had long idealized the United Nations and hoped to spearhead its peace-building work— actually coming true. At another level, it is the story of an innovative leader in a time of crisis, who forged new relationships with the stricken host city of New York in the shadow of 9/11, insisted on a strong stand against the terrorism that had assaulted it, and introduced new transition processes for the UN president that assured that in the future the General Assembly would not drift between annual sessions, when crisis and tragedy could at any time be looming.

The United Nations will never be the same in the wake of the momentous 56th General Assembly of 2001. The Reischauer Center is honored to present this historic chronicle by the Assembly's creative, distinguished leader in those difficult days. Dr. Han Seung-soo will be remembered both as a visionary and as a builder of future structures for a world that even he could not foresee.

Acknowledgments

Very few people know what really goes on in the corridors of the United Nations General Assembly as well as in and around the Office of its President.

I have always wondered why, while there were memoirs by all the Secretaries-General of the United Nations, no Presidents of the General Assembly have left any written record of their work at the United Nations. While carrying out the responsibilities of the presidency myself, I found that it was difficult for the President to record the activities and the stories behind the walls of the General Assembly. One reason for this is that the President is usually a cabinet minister at home or occupies a similar post that keeps him too busy and engaged in domestic affairs to concentrate and write on the work of the United Nations General Assembly. Also, while the Secretary-General usually serves two consecutive terms in office, with each term being five years, the President serves for only one year and does not make vital, newsworthy decisions that directly affect the lives of millions of people around the world.

I wanted to rectify this unbalanced situation by recording in a diary the everyday activities of my presidency. Based on that diary, I wrote a longer memoir while visiting the National Graduate Institute for Policy Studies (GRIPS) in Tokyo as a Senior Fellow during 2004–06. This is an abridged version of my memoir, translated from Japanese.

It is with pride and confidence that I am able to tell readers that our work at the United Nations General Assembly received generous appreciation and favorable comments from the diplomatic community in New York. This would not have been possible had I not been privileged with the devoted assistance of the members of my efficient cabinet, especially that of Ambassador Ban Ki-moon, currently the Secretary-General of the United Nations, Ambassador Oh Joon, currently at the Permanent Mission of the Republic of Korea to the United Nations, who checked and rechecked the manuscript for accuracy, and Counselor Yoon Yeo-cheol, currently Special Assistant to the Secretary-General, to whom I am eternally grateful.

I would like to take this opportunity to express my deep appreciation to President Toru Yoshimura of GRIPS for giving me the opportunity to concentrate on writing in Tokyo soon after I left domestic politics in 2004. Professor Atsushi Sunami and many other colleagues at GRIPS kindly provided me with academic hospitality. Ms. Naoko Yasumi provided a very efficient secretarial service during my stay at the Roppongi campus, and Ms. Masako Muto arranged equally professional service at the Toranomon office. Above all, I must give thanks to Professor Toshimitsu Shigemura of Waseda University School of International Studies for his translation of my memoir from Korean into Japanese. Despite being one of the busiest journalists-turned-professors in Japan, he volunteered for the translation.

My sincere gratitude also goes to Dr. Kim Young-moo and Ambassador Hyun Hong-choo of Kim & Chang Law Office in Seoul for their support and encouragement. I would also like to acknowledge the hard work and dedication of Dr. Min Sun-shik and Mr. Steven A. Stupak of YBM in Seoul who have done an excellent job of smoothing out the translation with utmost efficiency and professionalism.

Last, but not least, I would like to thank Professor Kent Calder, Director of the Reischauer Center at the Johns Hopkins University's School of Advanced International Studies (SAIS) in Washington, D.C., who was kind enough to suggest the translation of my memoir into English and has done a lot of work organizing the translation service and book-publishing. My memoir owes its greatest debt to him, and without his enthusiasm and support, it would not have been possible to publish the memoir in the United States. Working together with Professor Kent E. Calder, Ms. Akiko Imai, Ms. Izumi Sano, Mr. Andrew Gebert, Ms. Rie Tsumura, and all of the people at Automated Graphic Systems, Inc., provided invaluable services in translating as well as editing the manuscript, for which I am greatly indebted.

While I was in Japan writing my memoir, I had two of the happiest moments of my life, as Jiwoo, my grandson, was born to my son and daughter-in-law, Sangjun and Heehyun, and Jeongmin, my granddaughter, to my daughter and son-in-law, Sangeun and Seyeon. I have faith that the United Nations will offer as much hope to their generation as it did ours.

Han Seung-soo Biography

Han Seung-soo is currently Special Envoy of the UN Secretary-General on Climate Change and President of the Korea Water Forum. He has also recently served as Chairman of the PyeongChang Olympic Games Bid Committee and had an illustrious 16-year career in politics and government. He was a three-term Member of the Korean National Assembly, having been first elected in his hometown of Chuncheon, Gangwon-do Province, in April 1988.

Dr. Han served as President of the 56th Session of the United Nations General Assembly (2001–02). He also served as Korea's Minister of Foreign Affairs and Trade (2001–02), Deputy Prime Minister, and Minister of Finance and Economy (1996–97), Chief of Staff to the President of the Republic of Korea (1994–95), Korean Ambassador to the United States (1993–94), and Minister of Trade and Industry (1988–90).

The day of his inauguration (11 September 2001) as President of the United Nations General Assembly began amid crisis and confusion, stemming from the shocking terrorist attacks on the United States. He assumed the presidency of the General Assembly at the height of this turmoil, just one day after this historical upheaval. However, he successfully managed the General Debate and other important events, including a Special Session on Children. He strengthened the political will of the international community in dealing with such issues as international terrorism, conflict prevention, poverty eradication, HIV/AIDs, the digital divide, sustainable development, and the Millennium Goals. It was under his

1

Presidency that the rules of procedure were amended for the first time within the context of revitalizing and strengthening the role of the General Assembly of the United Nations. Together with Mr. Kofi Annan, Secretary-General of the United Nations, Dr. Han had the honor of representing the United Nations to receive the Nobel Peace Prize on December 10, 2001.

As Minister of Foreign Affairs and Trade, he was able to broaden the diplomatic horizon of Korea's foreign policy and contributed particularly to strengthening the strained Korea-US relations after the unsuccessful summit meeting between Presidents Kim Dae-jung and George W. Bush in early March 2001. He played a leading role in furthering the policy of peace and reconciliation on the Korean Peninsula. It was during this period, in May 2001, that the Swedish Prime Minister, in his capacity as President of the European Union, made his groundbreaking visit to Seoul and Pyongyang. Dr. Han contributed to addressing the challenge of international terrorism in various ways, such as participating in the Tokyo Conference on Reconstruction Assistance to Afghanistan, held in January 2002. He was chosen in 2001 by the World Economic Forum as Foreign Minister of the fourth annual Dream Cabinet, together with US Secretary of State Colin Powell.

As Deputy Prime Minister and Minister of Finance and Economy, Dr. Han was the nation's chief economic policy-maker. He was the principal minister who oversaw the negotiations for the accession of the Republic of Korea to the Organization for Economic Co-operation and Development (OECD) in 1996. Thus, he played a major role in opening and internationalizing Korea's capital market. Foreseeing the important role that venture businesses would play in the country's economy in the twenty-first century, he initiated and actively promoted legislation on the incentive stock option system and the technology-based KOSDAQ stock market.

As Chief of Staff to the President, Dr. Han assisted the President in carrying out outward-looking reform programs in all fields of national policy. It was during this period that local elections took place in Korea, restoring local autonomy for the first time in 35 years. It was during this period that the first offer of economic assistance, on a humanitarian basis, was made to North Korea in the form of rice. He was instrumental in coordinating a close working relationship between the Office of President and the Cabinet, which, when launched in December 1994, was instantly nicknamed the "Globalization Cabinet."

As Korean Ambassador to the United States, Dr. Han was heavily involved in the resolution of North Korean nuclear issues. In 1993, he was posted to Washington, D.C. about a month after North Korea declared that it intended to withdraw from the Nuclear Non-Proliferation Treaty (NPT). He worked closely with the US delegation to produce the Geneva Agreed Framework in October 1994. He was also able to settle many difficult problems that Korean-Americans faced when they wanted to become US citizens.

As Minister of Trade and Industry, he was instrumental in the successful Super 301 negotiations with the United States and helped launch Korea on a path toward a new trade relationship with the United States and other countries. It was through the successful negotiations over Super 301 that Korea was cleared of a negative image as an unfair trading nation. In 1989, Dr. Han was one of the initiators of the Asia-Pacific Economic Cooperation (APEC), a forum now held annually among Asia-Pacific countries to discuss ways to promote economic cooperation in the region. He initiated the Taejeon International Exposition in 1993, which was the first Expo to be held in a country not yet fully industrialized. He founded the Korea Academy of Industrial Technology (KAITEC) in 1989, aimed at expanding the technological basis of small and medium-sized enterprises. He also succeeded in rationalizing the shipping industry.

Before he entered politics in 1988, Dr. Han had a long and distinguished academic career as Professor of Economics at Seoul National University (1970–88). He was Research Officer at the Department of Applied Economics, University of Cambridge and Emmanuel College (1968–70), Cambridge and Lecturer and Fellow in Economics at the University of York (1965–68), York, England. He was Visiting Professor at the Faculty of Liberal Arts and Sciences, University of Tokyo (1986–87), Tokyo, Japan and Senior Fulbright Scholar at the Department of Economics, Harvard University (1985–86), Cambridge, MA, USA.

Educated at Yonsei University (BA) and Seoul National University (MPA), he obtained his doctorate in economics from the University of York (Ph.D. 1968), York, England, where he was also awarded an honorary Doctor of the University in 1997. He is a recipient of honorary doctorates from Yonsei University and Kangwon National University. Dr. Han's doctoral thesis, *The Growth and Function of the European Budget*, was awarded the 6th European Communities Prize (economics section) in 1971 by the Commission of the European Communities as the best doctoral thesis written on European integration during 1967–69.

It was a first attempt to develop a theory of supra-national budgets, which was then applied to analyze the economic impact of the budget of the Commission of the European Communities.

From 1987 to 1988, Dr. Han served as the first Chairman of the Korea Trade Commission and worked as a member of the Commissions on Tax Reform, Bank Reform, and Tariff Reform, all set up by the Ministry of Finance during the 1980s. Before joining the government, he served as advisor to several public and private-sector organizations, including the Bank of Korea, where he later served as Chairman of the Monetary Board, when he held the post of Finance Minister, the Korea Export-Import Bank, Korea Industrial Bank, Korea Chamber of Commerce and Industry, Federation of Korean Industries, and the Korea International Trade Association. He also worked as a consultant to the World Bank and UNESCAP. He was seconded by the World Bank to serve as Financial Advisor to the Government of Jordan from 1974 to 1976. During his academic career, he visited many foreign universities, including the University of Paris I (Panthéon-Sorbonne) during the early 1980s, to give seminars. After his retirement from politics, he spent two years as Senior Fellow at the National Graduate Institute for Policy Studies in Tokyo during 2004–06.

Han Seung-soo has been widely decorated both at home and abroad, including the Order of Public Service Merit (blue stripes, 1990) and the Order of Diplomatic Service Merit (*gwanghwajang*, 2004) by the Korean Government, Grand-Crois de L'Ordre de la Couronne (1989) from Belgium, Orden Mexicana del Aguila Azteca, Grado Collar (2001) from

5

Mexico, and an honorary knighthood (KBE) from HM Queen Elizabeth II of the United Kingdom in 2004. He was the first recipient of the Columbia Law School/Parker School Award for Distinguished International Service in 1997.

Dr. Han has written many professional articles, both in Korean and English, and several publications, including *The 'New' Theory of Economic Policy* (Korean, 1996), *The Theory of Economic Policy* (Korean, 1994), *Social Welfare in Britain* (Korean, 1979), *The Economics of the Middle East; Foundation of Arab Renaissance* (Korean, 1997), *The Health of Nations* (Seoul Computer Press, Seoul, 1985), *Tax Harmonisation in Britain and the EEC* (PEP & Chatham House, London, 1968, co-authored), *Britain and the Common Market; Effect of Entry on the Pattern of Manufacturing Production* (Cambridge University Press, Cambridge, 1971, co-authored), and others.

Dr. Han is currently Chairman of the Board, Gangwon Information and Multimedia Corporation, Chairman, Onggi Scholarship Foundation, Senior Advisor, Kim & Chang, President, Korea-UK Forum for the Future, and Board Member, Yonsei University Foundation, Metlife Welfare Foundation, and Keumkang Scholarship Foundation. His hobbies include mountain hiking, playing *baduk* (5th *dan*, Japanese go), and collecting biographies. He is married with two children.

6

Chapter 1: September 11th and United Nations' Response

The World Trade Center Is Burning

On 11 September 2001, New York City was blessed with a clear autumn sky. On that day I, Korea's Foreign Minister, was slated to be formally elected President of the 56th Session of the United Nations General Assembly. I knew that it would be a challenge to balance my responsibilities of President while fulfilling those of Foreign Minister, but I had no way of knowing how intense and difficult the political and diplomatic maneuverings at the United Nations would become.

I awoke before dawn, feeling the weight of the responsibility I was about to take on. I was moved by the sight of the sun rising above the horizon, as if to celebrate a new departure. The future looked bright and hopeful. In the crisp autumn air, the morning sun seemed to proudly shed its rays on a tranquil world. Looking back, it now seems that these rays were actually expressing concern for our future. Who would have expected that this day would become a day of tragedy and change the course of history?

In retrospect, September 11 marked the start of a tumultuous year during which I would be tossed about by the rough waves of international politics. I witnessed the dedication and commitment of many worthy world leaders and UN officers who risked their lives to restore peace and security to the world. I will never forget the noble sacrifice of my UN colleagues who lost their lives in Iraq.

In December 2001, I had the honor of accepting the

Nobel Peace Prize on behalf of the United Nations. I devoted my energies to the reform of the Security Council and the revitalization of the General Assembly. I took several major tours, including one to Africa. One year may seem like a short time, but I felt that during that brief period I achieved the work of several years.

It had been a tradition to inaugurate the President of the General Assembly at the opening meeting of the General Assembly in September, for a term of one year. On the morning of the new session, an International Prayer Breakfast is held in honor of the new President. The breakfast ceremony began at 8:00 AM that morning. My wife and I were seated with the outgoing President, former Finnish Prime Minister Harri Holkeri, and his wife. It was the first time a Korean was to be elected President of the UN General Assembly, and the organizers had invited Korean singers and musicians to perform and sing hymns.

The ceremony was scheduled to end slightly after 9:00. At 9:30 AM, I was scheduled to join Secretary-General Kofi Annan in another ritual, the ringing of the Peace Bell in front of the UN building. The Japanese Government donated the Peace Bell to the UN in 1954.

The International Prayer Breakfast took more time than usual, and the time to ring the Peace Bell was rapidly approaching. There was an air of anxiety in the room. At that moment, a UN staff member rushed into the room with a tense expression on his face. He whispered something to Ambassador Ban Ki-moon, who had been appointed as my Chef de Cabinet. Ban looked stricken for a moment, but gaining his composure, jotted something on a piece of paper and rushed over to me. His face was drawn and stern.

8

"The World Trade Center is burning."

An incident beyond imagination was taking place just a few miles south of the UN Headquarters. On the very day when the 56th Session of the United Nations General Assembly was to open, an event symbolic of peace and international cooperation, two hijacked US passenger planes were deliberately crashed into the World Trade Center. No words could describe the shock that gripped people at the United Nations and throughout the United States.

The opening of the annual session and the inauguration ceremony of the President were originally scheduled to take place that day at 3:00 PM, but everything had to be postponed. Making matters worse, all phone lines in New York City had gone down. The telecommunications back-up system, located in the World Trade Center, had been destroyed along with the building. All lines of communication to the outside world were severed. New York City was cut off from the rest of the world.

Instructions were given for the UN staff to evacuate the headquarters building after we were informed that the UN Headquarters was a likely target for further terrorist attacks. Because the election for the presidency of the General Assembly had not been held, a temporary office was set up for me inside the Permanent Mission of the Republic of Korea to the United Nations at 335 E. 45th Street. The ad hoc office of the President-designate was soon ready for its longest day of operation.

In the face of this challenge to the world, it was urgent that the functioning of the United Nations be restored to normal as quickly as possible. One of the most pressing questions before us was when to open the 56th annual session of the General Assembly.

9

Mr. Chen Jian, Under Secretary-General for General Assembly Affairs, Mr. Vadim Perfiliev, Deputy Director of General Assembly and ECOSOC Affairs Division, Mr. Ozdinch Mustafa, Chief of General Assembly Servicing Branch, and other staff members of the Secretariat came to my office to discuss this issue. Secretary-General Kofi Annan was resolutely committed to opening the session the next day. I felt his strong resolve to show the world, as quickly as possible, that the United Nations was standing unaffected by the incident. While I fully shared the Secretary-General's resolve, no one could guarantee that we would be able to return the UN to its normal state and operate tomorrow as it had yesterday.

That night New York was gripped by fear, isolated from the rest of the world. All land routes into Manhattan were closed. Neither cars nor pedestrians were allowed into the city. After the collapse of the World Trade Center buildings, Manhattan was filled with dust, smoke, and an unpleasant, acrid odor. This was especially pronounced on First Avenue between 43rd and 48th Streets, where the UN Headquarters is located. For security reasons, all cars were forbidden entry to the streets approaching the UN. Dump trucks carrying loads of large rocks and sand blocked the streets leading to the UN Headquarters, and a large steel-frame security door was brought down, closing off access to the building's underground parking facility.

Throughout the day, it was impossible to walk the streets of New York without covering our mouths and noses with a handkerchief. The winds blowing from the southwest brought a pungent odor that assaulted the senses. The windows of virtually all of the city's apartment buildings were shut tightly. People felt lost and abandoned in the heart of the city.

Amidst the confusion, there emerged a powerful will to re-store peace and order to the city. Underlying the chaos and de-spair filling New York, I could not help but feel people's strong hope and desire to see the United Nations functioning. The Office of the President of the General Assembly and the Executive Office of the Secretary-General affirmed their intention to open the UN General Assembly on 12 September 2001 at 3:00 PM and elect the President of the General Assembly, whatever the circumstances.

September 11, 2001, was a nightmarish day in the history of the United Nations. It was symbolic of this that, for the first time in 56 years, the General Assembly President's seat was va-cant for one full day.

Electing the President of the United Nations General Assembly

The next morning, under the strictest security, I was picked up by the General Assembly President's car. Mr. Peter Yevoli, the UN security agent specially assigned to the General Assembly President, came to escort me from my apartment and usher me to my office at A200 in the United Nations Headquarters. I arrived at 9:00 AM

The President's Office is located on the 2nd floor of the headquarters building. The windows of the office open onto a stunning, panoramic view of the East River and New York City's outer boroughs of Queens and Brooklyn. For many years, the Office of the President of the United Nations General Assembly had been located on the 38th floor of the headquarters building. However, I was told that some 10 years earlier tensions arose between the Secretary-General and the President of the General Assembly. As a result, when it was time for the presidency to be turned over, the Secretary-

General decided to relocate the President's Office from the 38th floor to the 2nd floor.

In light of this history, I could have demanded to re-establish the President's Office on the 38th floor of the headquarters building. In June 2001, after I was nominated to assume the presidency, I had occasion to visit the President's Office. After much consideration, I decided to continue using the present office. It was, however, too small for our needs, so I requested that the office be expanded to make more space for my cabinet staff.

Among the reasons I decided to keep the office in that location was its proximity to the General Assembly Hall and, frankly, I enjoyed the view. I also felt that keeping a certain physical distance from the Secretary-General might help us maintain a better working relationship. I could not suppress my disappointment that it had not been possible to start work in this newly renovated Office of the President on the previous day, as scheduled.

Even on 12 September the situation remained tense. As soon as I arrived at my office, while I was still trying to catch my breath, a security officer rushed in and urgently insisted that I move to an underground floor.

"According to information from the United States Government, terrorists have plans to attack the UN Headquarters today," he said.

With security guards protecting me front and rear, I walked at a deliberate pace to the basement shelter. I must admit that I did not feel entirely confident. Later, as I prayed, I remembered the faces of my friends and supporters in my hometown and of the people of Korea. September 11 was to be celebrated as Han Seung-soo Day in my hometown of Chuncheon, which I had represented as Member of the National Assembly since April 1988. My thoughts traveled to Chuncheon and to the people of the town where I had spent my youth. All I could do was let them know that I was alive and that they should not be overly concerned for my well-being. I was touched when I thought about my friends and supporters back home.

At that time, I did not know that throughout the day the Korean TV networks were streaming "Foreign Minister Han Seung-soo's safety has been confirmed" across the news tickers on TV screens. When I later learned of this, I was deeply moved and filled with a profound sense of gratitude.

In the underground shelter of the United Nations Headquarters, I spoke with Secretary-General Annan. We agreed that regardless of any information the United States Government might receive, we had to open the General Assembly in the afternoon, elect the President, and show the world that the United Nations was present and in operation. We both felt this was crucial. We could not allow the world to think that the United Nations had been intimidated or driven to inaction by a terrorist act.

The situation outside of UN Headquarters was severe beyond our imagination. There were various rumors and alerts about possible terrorist attacks against the United Nations. All streets leading to UN Headquarters were blocked. Security was so tight that I felt not even a mouse could get through.

Friends and acquaintances who had been planning to attend the inauguration ceremony could not reach New York because all international and domestic airlines and railways had ceased operation. My friends from Seoul, Tokyo, and cities in the United States were held up at airports in Toronto, Chicago, and elsewhere, while others were stranded on a train in the Philadelphia station. No one could get close to New York.

Despite all this, the United Nations General Assembly opened its 56th Session at 3:00 PM on 12 September 2001. Former Finnish Prime Minister Holkeri, President of the 55th UN General Assembly and now Temporary President, took his place in the President's seat and announced the opening of the session. Secretary-General Kofi Annan was seated to his right. On his left was Under Secretary-General for General Assembly Affairs Chen Jian, former Ambassador of China to Japan.

President Holkeri, after declaring the 56th Session of the General Assembly open, expressed his deepest condolences to the people and the government of the United States for the tragic loss of life resulting from the previous day's terrorist acts. After observing one minute of prayer, President Holkeri moved on to the election of the President of the General Assembly. He declared,

> I now invite members of the General Assembly to proceed to the election of the President of the General Assembly at its fifty-sixth session. May I recall that, in accordance with paragraph 1 of the annex to General Assembly resolution 33/138, the President of the General Assembly at the fifty-sixth session should be elected from among the Asian States. In this connection, I have been informed by the Chairman of the Group of Asian States that the group has endorsed the candidacy of His Excellency Mr. Han Seung-soo of the Republic of Korea for the presidency of the General Assembly. Taking into account the provisions of paragraph 16 of annex VI to the rules of procedure, I therefore declare His Excellency Mr. Han Seung-soo of the Republic of Korea elected by acclamation President of the General Assembly at its fifty-sixth session. I extend my sincere congratulations to His Excellency Mr. Han

Seung-soo and I invite him to assume the presidency. I request the Chief of Protocol to escort the President to the podium.

With this, the hall was filled with a resounding applause. I was elected President of the 56th Session of the United Nations General Assembly by acclamation. From D-11, the seat of the delegation of the Republic of Korea in the General Assembly Hall, I was escorted by the UN Chief of Protocol, Ms. Nadia Younes (tragically killed in the 19 August 2003 attack on the UN headquarters in Baghdad). I walked toward the podium and received the President's gavel from Mr. Holkeri.

Looking back, the process in Korea that resulted in my being elected President of the General Assembly had been difficult. There were voices critically questioning whether it was right for a Foreign Minister to be absent from Seoul for protracted periods of time.

However, through painstaking efforts, it was finally possible to persuade those who opposed the nomination of a Foreign Minister to the post of the President of the United Nations General Assembly. The following corroborating data were presented to convince President Kim Dae-jung and those concerned in the President's Office:

1. Past cases of Foreign Ministers of Member States simultaneously holding the position of the President of the General Assembly

2. Evidence that in recent years it had become common practice for a Foreign Minister to hold a dual position as the President of the General Assembly

3. The work program of the President is concentrated in the period from September to December, thus enabling

schedule coordination between the United Nations and domestic tasks

4. The number of days during the year that the Presidents actually spent in New York to attend the affairs of the General Assembly

Up to that point, having already occupied a variety of major public positions in Korea, including Minister of Trade and Industry, Ambassador to the United States, Chief of Staff to the President, Deputy Prime Minister, and Minister of Finance, I did not find another cabinet post especially attractive. I agreed to take the position in the hope that my experience in foreign policy would enable me to better serve my country at a critical time when tensions in Korea-US relations seemed to be increasing. In contrast, I had long felt a special sense of mission and determination to serve as the President of the United Nations General Assembly.

The President is elected from among Member States for one year on a regionally rotating basis. In 2001 it was the turn of the Asian group to take the presidency. Korea's candidacy was supported by all other Asian Member States. After this Korean presidency, it would theoretically take 180 or so years until the next opportunity for another Korean to assume the presidency, as each Member State is entitled to occupy the post. There were 189 Member States in the United Nations General Assembly in 2001.

I felt that this was a chance that God had given me and that it was no coincidence that I was appointed Foreign Minister at this critical juncture in history. I had a clear desire to become the President of the General Assembly. I told the National Security Advisor to the President, who happened to

Addressing the opening of the General Assembly's fifty-sixth session on 12 September 2001, soon after my election as President, flanked by Secretary-General Kofi Annan, left, and Under Secretary-General for General Assembly Affairs and Conference Services Chen Jian.
© UN/DPI
Photo by Eskinder Debebe

Annual Interfaith Service of Commitment to the Work of the United Nations at St. Bartholomew's Church in New York on 13 September 2001.
© UN/DPI
Photo by Eskinder Debebe

Speaking before the Ringing of the Peace Bell on 14 September 2001.
© UN/DPI
Photo by Eskinder Debebe

Rudolph Giuliani, walking toward the podium, became the first New York mayor
in nearly 50 years to address the United Nations. Seated at the podium are,
from left, Secretary-General Annan, myself, and Under Secretary-General for
General Assembly Affairs and Conference Services Chen Jian (October 2001).
© UN/DPI
Photo by Evan Schneider

Meeting with the Chairmen of Regional Groups on 2 October 2001.
© UN/DPI
Photo by Eskinder Debebe

Meeting with Nobel Peace Prize Laureates on 8 October 2001.
© UN/DPI
Photo by Tara Engberg

Observance of UN Day at Headquarters with Indian Performers, my wife Soja, and Mr. and Mrs. Kofi Annan (October 2001).
© UN/DPI
Photo by Eskinder Debebe

Meeting of Six Principal Organs of the United Nations on 30 October 2001.
© UN/DPI
Photo by Evan Schneider

President George W. Bush addressing the General Assembly on 10 November 2001.
© UN/DPI
Photo by Tara Engberg

Members of Nobel Peace Committee with the laureates and their wives at the cocktail
before the "Little Dinner" (December 2001).
© Nobel Peace Committee

Entering the City Hall to receive the Nobel Peace Prize with Mr. Kofi Annan to my left (December 2001).
© Nobel Peace Committee

Receiving the Nobel Peace Prize from Gunnar Berge, Chairman of the Norwegian Nobel Committee (December 2001).
© Pressens Bild
Photo by Heiko Junge, AP Photo

Reception after the Nobel Peace Prize Ceremony by HM King Harald V and the royal family in the palace (December 2001).
© Nobel Peace Committee

At a reception before the Nobel Peace Prize dinner and banquet with Mr. and Mrs. Kofi Annan and my wife Soja (December 2001).
© Nobel Peace Committee

Members of the Nobel Peace Committee with laureates and their wives in the room where the pictures of past laureates are on display (December 2001).
© Nobel Peace Committee

Commemorating International Women's Day at UN Headquarters with Shashi Tharoor, interim head of the UN Department of Public Information, left, and US First Lady Laura Bush (March 2002).
© UN/DPI
Photo by Eskinder Debebe

Meeting with Council of the Presidents of the UN General Assembly (May 2002).

Meeting with Pope John Paul II in the Vatican with my wife Soja to my left and
Ambassador and Mrs. Ban Ki-moon far right behind the Pope (June 2002).
© Fotografia Felici, Roma

My wife Soja receiving a rosary from Pope John Paul II in the Vatican (June 2002).
© Fotografia Felici, Roma

President Abdoulaye Wade of Senegal, keynote speaker at the Plenary Session on the
Digital Divide, on 17 July 2002.
© UN/DPI
Photo by Eskinder Debebe

In front of the Office of the President of the 56th session of the UN General Assembly with Ambassador Ban Ki-moon, Chef de Cabinet, Eighth Secretary-General (to my left), and other staff (September 2002).
© UN/DPI
Photo by Evan Schneider

The day I left the United Nations; in front of the General Assembly with national flags in the background (September 2002).
© Photo privately taken

With my wife Soja and Ambassador and Mrs. Ban Ki-moon in the General Assembly Hall the day before I left the UN (September 2002).
Photo privately taken

Members of Staff at the Offices of the President and of the Under Secretary-General for General Assembly Affairs: Under Secretary-General Chen Jian, to my right; Ambassador Ban Ki-moon, third to my right; my wife Soja; and Mrs. Ban, to my left.
Photo privately taken

be one of my former students at Seoul National University, "If you ask me to choose between being the President of the United Nations General Assembly and being the Foreign Minister of Korea, I will, without hesitation, choose the former. " I cannot forget the look of disbelief on his face. He could not conceive of how a Korean politician would relinquish the position of Foreign Minister to take up the post of President at the United Nations General Assembly for a term of only one year.

For Koreans, the United Nations Represented Hope for Peace

How can I best explain my determination to become the President of the United Nations General Assembly? From childhood, the United Nations had been the embodiment of my hopes and dreams. Although Korea had won independence from Japan in 1945, the nation then had to suffer the tragedy of being divided into South and North. The people of the two Koreas, sharing a common national and cultural heritage, yet separated by ideology, fought in the Korean War (1950–53). While enduring this tragedy, the only source of hope for the citizens of South Korea was the United Nations.

Soon after the division of Korea, and in the midst of the emerging cold war rivalry, South Korea attempted to establish an independent government through free elections. The United Nations supported South Korea's request. Resolution 112 (II)-B[1] was adopted by the General Assembly on 14 November 1947 to form the UN Temporary Commission on Korea (UNTCOK). The Commission had the mandate of ensuring that the election of the National Assembly was conducted in a fair and transparent manner. After the successful general election, the Republic of Korea was born on 15 August 1948 and the United Nations General Assembly recognized it as the only legitimate government on the Korean Peninsula.

On 25 June 1950, the Korean War broke out when North Korean troops invaded the South. Had it not been for the support of the United Nations, South Korea might have ceased to exist as a state. On 27 June 1950, during a boycott by the Soviet Ambassador to the UN, the Security Council adopted Resolution 83 (S-1511); then, on 7 July of the same year, Resolution 164 (S-1588). On the basis of these two resolutions, 16 Member States entered the Korean War as part of the UN force, fighting for South Korea until the ceasefire of 27 July 1953.

As a child, I learned the names of the Presidents of the UN General Assembly during the Korean War. I was able to recite them from memory. The President of the 4th Session of the General Assembly during 1949–50 at the outbreak of the war was the first to be elected from Asia—Philippine Foreign Minister General Carlos Romulo. Romulo was a high-ranking officer known for his work on the staff of General Douglas MacArthur. During 1950–51, the President of the 5th Session was Mr. Nasrollah Entezam of Iran. The President of the 6th Session, 1951–52, was Mr. Luis Padilla Nerva of Mexico. During 1952–53, the President of the 7th Session was Mr. Lester B. Pearson, later to become the Prime Minister of Canada. The President of the 8th Session of the General Assembly during 1953–54 was the sister of Indian Prime Minister Jawaharlal Nehru, Mrs. Vijaya Lakshmi Pandit.

During the Korean War, on 7 October 1950, the United Nations General Assembly adopted Resolution 376 (V), establishing the United Nations Commission for the Unification and

Rehabilitation of Korea (UNCURK), which became the UN's leading institution in Korea to promote post-war reconstruction. Following the cease-fire in 1953, the United Nations continued to support Korea's economic growth and development through the United Nations Korean Reconstruction Agency (UNKRA).

As an expression of appreciation at having been saved by the United Nations, United Nations Day, 24 October—the day of the UN's founding—was designated a public holiday in Korea. "The Song of the United Nations," composed by a Korean, became popular and everyone knew the lyrics.

The United Nations Song   19

> *Spanning east and western hemispheres, six conti*
> *   nents and five oceans.*
> *Different races and peoples live in harmony, sharing*
> *   one heart.*
> *The spreading light, the ideals of the United Nations*
> *The flame of love shines on this land.*
> *U-N! U-N! U-N! Messenger of Peace, let us sing with*
> *   hands raised high. (repeat)*
>
> *On the sea, on the land, and in the skies*
> *Crusaders for justice fight with their lives*
> *Against evil domination, to thwart unjust ambitions.*
> *From this land where blood has flowed, flowers will*
> *   bloom.*

As children, we used to sing the UN song often. Whenever I sang it, I felt as if doves of peace were taking flight in my heart.

The UN Member States shipped relief aid to the people

of Korea, suffering from poverty and hunger. As we gazed up at the skies, we saw planes dispatched by the United Nations bringing valuable supplies to our land. The United Nations was our only source of hope and strength to persevere through the horrors of war.

Korean youth were excited to read articles about the UN resolutions or to listen to broadcasts of speeches about Korea given at the United Nations General Assembly. I am sure that among them there were many young people whose hearts were filled with the dream of some day becoming the President of the United Nations General Assembly. Indeed, as a young boy I cherished that dream.

When I was a child, my family lived deep in the countryside, surrounded by mountains, with no roads passable by car. Ours was an isolated village at the foot of a mountain. To attend junior and senior high schools in Chuncheon city, I had to get up at dawn and travel five kilometers on foot. Chuncheon is a mountainous region with many rivers and lakes. I had to take two ferries, crossing two rivers, to reach school. Despite this harsh environment, somewhere in my heart a strong desire was emerging to work for the United Nations one day and pay back the debt that Korea, as a nation, owed the United Nations.

On my way to and from school, I would occasionally pick up an English-language magazine discarded by the side of the road by American soldiers and trace on my palm the shape of the strange English letters, forming words. In running from one ferry to the other I would memorize the English words by saying them out loud, dreaming of one day becoming the President of the UN General Assembly, following in the footsteps of leaders like General Romulo, Prime Minister Pearson, and Mrs. Pandit.

In those days, the dream to someday lead the world by helping countries tormented by war, such as Korea, was only a childish fantasy. However, it was this great dream that offered one destitute boy the hope and sense of purpose needed to continue studying.

When I think back on those days, I cannot help but feel that my heart was yearning to accomplish something that was entirely unrealistic. Part of what enabled me to continue pursuing this dream was, in a word, my ignorance. Korea was not even a Member State of the United Nations; looking back, I have no reasonable explanation of why a boy living in a remote village in a country not even a Member State of the United Nations should have cherished the hope of someday becoming the President of the United Nations General Assembly.

Even if Korea became a Member State of the United Nations, its call to put forth a candidate for the President would come only in turn with the passing of a number of years equal to the number of Member States. Who could say when Korea's turn might come up? Moreover, should Korea's turn come up during my lifetime, what were the chances of my candidacy? The likelihood of my dream being realized was less than 1 in 1 billion. It would be virtually impossible.

Over the years, I did not give up my dream and, on 12 September 2001, that dream came true. On that day, apart from being very happy, I also felt the tremendous weight of the mission for world peace and development that had been entrusted to me.

Chapter 2:
Flower of the General Assembly—
General Debate

On 14 September, three days after the terrorist attacks, I convened the General Committee of the General Assembly. The General Committee is an important group that determines the agenda of the General Assembly. It is comprised of 28 members: the President and 21 Vice Presidents of the General Assembly, and six representatives from the Main Committees. The Main Committees are: Disarmament and International Security; Economic and Financial; Social, Humanitarian, and Cultural (responsible for human rights); Special Political and Decolonization; Administrative and Budgetary; and Legal.

The General Committee is convened at the start of the annual General Assembly session to decide vital matters such as the agenda, which includes the order in which speeches and statements will be made over the course of the session.

In times of heated disputes and conflicts the number of representatives who want to make statements before the General Assembly naturally increases. At such times, the General Committee may have to meet through the night to make scheduling adjustments. In the past, tensions between North and So uth Korea have often created such conditions.

In recent years, political debates have taken place concerning the issue of Taiwan. Some Member States supporting Taiwan had requested time to deliver speeches in which they called for Taiwan's recognition as a Member State of the UN.

China then worked to block such moves, and heated debates would occupy the time and energy of the General Committee, which would meet for long hours to deal with the matter.

Immediately after the General Committee had convened, I was informed that I had a phone call from US Secretary of State Colin Powell. I asked one of the Vice Presidents to take over chairing the committee and returned to my office to take his call.

Secretary Powell congratulated me on my election as the President of the United Nations General Assembly and expressed his appreciation for the Korean Government's prompt declaration of support for the United States in the wake of the terrorist attacks.

I expressed my condolences to the victims of the attacks and said, "Korea feels a strong sense of solidarity with the United States Government and will actively participate in efforts to eliminate terrorism."

After my conversation with Secretary Powell, I returned to the General Committee. Soon after, however, I was told that Secretary-General Annan needed to consult with me on a matter of urgency and wanted to meet me in my office. I suspected bad news. Annan, together with his Chef de Cabinet and four aides, came to my office. As I had expected, it was indeed bad news.

He sounded troubled. "I just talked to Mayor Giuliani. I was also contacted by the US State Department. Because of the 9/11 terror attacks, security is stretched thin. There are not enough security staff to protect the Heads of State and Government who will be attending the General Assembly. They cannot promise a sufficient level of security until the end of October. How shall we deal with this?"

Nothing like this had happened in the history of the United Nations. Annan and I discussed how to handle the General Debate under these circumstances.

When we spoke moments earlier, Secretary Powell had made no mention of any security problem. I figured that this type of problem was probably handled by working-level State Department officials and would not have been reported directly to the Secretary of State.

The most important meeting over the course of the General Assembly is the General Debate, where the Heads of State or Government address the body. Although the session is called "General Debate," no debate actually takes place. Heads of State or Government, or their representatives, deliver general statements that sum up the states' foreign policy. To convey its actual role, this part of the Assembly should probably be called "Keynote Addresses."

The General Debate is attended by monarchs, presidents, and other Heads of State who are invited to deliver speeches. When a Head of State does not attend, he or she may be represented by the prime minister, foreign minister, or other cabinet-level official. Heads of State or Government often use their visit to the United Nations as an opportunity for summit diplomacy. Many seek meetings with the US President or Secretary of State; for example, bilateral meetings such as a US-Japan summit, US-China or US-Korea foreign ministerial meetings. Out of the entire year, this period represents the peak season for diplomacy at the United Nations.

Scheduling the General Debate

Secretary-General Annan and I discussed three possibilities for the General Debate:

1. There would be no General Debate at the 56th Session of the United Nations General Assembly.
2. The General Debate would take place, but because of the lack of security, speakers would be restricted to the heads of the UN Mission of the respective Member States.
3. The General Debate would be postponed until the security problem could be resolved adequately to permit the participation of Heads of State and Government.

Although Secretary-General Annan indicated that he would respect my wishes, he suggested the third option as his preference. He emphasized that Heads of State and Government look forward to speaking at the United Nations once a year. It is a great opportunity for them to express their national interests and clarify their policy stances to both domestic and international audiences. If this opportunity were lost, Annan emphasized, it would undermine their appreciation for the role of the United Nations.

I could understand Annan's position; since the General Debate represents an unparalleled opportunity to meet and discuss important issues with world leaders, he did not wish to cancel it. When I think about it, that desire was possibly even stronger in me. My term as the General Assembly President was for only one year. This would be my first and only opportunity to engage in discussions with the various Heads of State and Government. I wanted to directly talk to these leaders who were shaping the course of the world and learn from their experiences. In that regard, Annan and I shared a similar view on the matter.

The General Debate of the 56th annual session was originally scheduled to take place from 24 September to

5 October. It is customary for the dates to be determined at the end of the previous session. Based on my consultation with the Secretary-General, I followed procedure and convened a meeting with the chairs of the five regional groups. Fortunately, all of the regional-group chairs agreed on option three. The following Monday, 17 September, the chairs of the regional groups would poll their members in preparation for resuming discussions on 18 September on the General Debate issue.

As I was scheduled to be in Washington, D.C. on 18 September for a Korea-US Foreign Ministerial meeting with Secretary Powell, I had to ask my Chef de Cabinet, Ambassador Ban Ki-moon, to chair the regional-group meeting. Later that day, Ban informed me of the good news that the Member States had reached a consensus to support option three.

This was the first piece of business I took care of as the President of the General Assembly. Under the circumstances, we could not be certain that we would even be able to hold the General Debate, but we could not leave the dates undecided. I devised a contingency plan.

I felt it was important that we discuss the details for holding the General Debate and set a tentative schedule. On 20 September, I convened a meeting with the Vice Presidents. There are 21 Vice Presidents in the General Assembly, including representatives of the five permanent members of the Security Council.

They were, from the five permanent member states, Ambassador James Cunningham (USA), Ambassador Sir Jeremy Greenstock (UK), Ambassador Jean-David Levitte (France), Ambassador Wang Yingang (China), and Ambassador

Sergey Lavrov (Russia); from Asian states, Ambassador Ouch Bortih (Cambodia), Ambassador Fawzi Bin Abdul Majeed Shobokshi (Saudi Arabia), Ambassador Murari Raj Sharma (Nepal), and Ambassador Kamil M. Baialinov (Kyrgyzstan); from East European states, Ambassador Ion Botnaru (Moldova); from West European states, Ambassador Elias Gounaris (Greece) and Ambassador Walter Balzan (Malta); from African states, Ambassador Jagdish Koonjul (Mauritania), Ambassador Ibrahim Mbaba Kamara (Sierra Leone), Ambassador Abuzed Omar Dorda (Libya), Ambassador Dumisani Shadrack Kumalo (South Africa), Ambassador Baile Ikouebe (Congo), and Ambassador Abdul Mejid Hussein (Ethiopia); and from Latin American and Caribbean states, Ambassador Eladio Loizaga (Paraguay), Ambassador Eduardo J. Sevilla Somoza (Nicaragua), and Ambassador Gert Rosenthal (Guatemala).

This was a very unusual gathering. Meetings of the Vice Presidents are usually a formality. They almost never become a substitute forum where issues of importance are discussed or debated. In this meeting, however, we discussed an issue of great magnitude—the timing for holding the General Debate. In the 56 years of United Nations history, this was the first time keynote speeches by Heads of State and Government were not held as scheduled.

Was October a possibility? Mayor Giuliani had indicated that October might be difficult. In that case our next choice would be November, although because of schedule conflicts with other important international events, the prospects for holding the General Debate in November were not bright. The Commonwealth Meeting was to take place in early November. The ASEAN+3 Conference would be held in Brunei on 5–6

November, and the Islamic month of Ramadan was to begin on 17 November. In the United States, Thanksgiving fell on Thursday, 22 November. It seemed impossible to secure two unbroken weeks in November for the General Debate.

I therefore proposed that we hold the session for seven days, 10–16 November, working through the weekend. Since we would have less than the usual two weeks, we would be forced to make adjustments to the program and the time allocated for each speech.

My proposal was to hold the General Debate for eight hours each day from 9:00 AM to 1:00 PM and from 3:00 PM to 7:00 PM The time allocated each day for General Debate is normally six hours: from 10:00 AM to 1:00 PM and from 3:00 PM to 6:00 PM I also felt that we would have to reduce the time allotted to each speech from 20 to 15 minutes.

The 21 Vice Presidents voiced their unanimous acceptance of this proposal, although I was still concerned about whether the representatives of all the Member States would agree to the changes. Even if we were able to open the session on Saturday, 10 November, we still had to resolve the important question of whether US President Bush would be able to attend the opening. It was a tradition to have the President of the United States address the General Assembly on the first day of the session.

I contacted US Ambassador John Negroponte and asked him to confirm the matter with the White House. I also asked the chairman of each regional group to secure the consensus of their Member States with regard to the new contingency plan.

The Asian regional group, to which I belonged, raised objections to it. The chairman of the Asian group, the Ambassador of Vietnam, informed me that the Arab nations objected to the proposal. This was a serious challenge that, as I saw it, threatened to undermine the standing of the President of the General Assembly. If the President could not convince the Member States of his own group, how could he expect to convince the other regional groups?

The Vietnamese Ambassador explained that the Fourth World Trade Organization (WTO) Ministerial Conference was to be held in Doha, Qatar, from 9 to 14 November and that the Arab nations had therefore requested these dates be avoided. They also demanded that the time allocated for speeches be kept at 20 minutes, as usual. Further, even if it meant holding the session during Ramadan, they wanted the two-week timeframe maintained, following the precedent of past years.

Not only was I disappointed by this reaction, but somewhat annoyed and frustrated. They seemed to have no idea of the difficulty I had gone through to come up with this proposal. It did not seem unreasonable to expect that the chair of the group would be able to persuade the Arab nations. Why could the members of the Asian group not show more respect for the President who had been nominated from among their number? Protocol prevented me from expressing my irritation.

Initially, I considered avoiding the dates of the WTO Ministerial Conference and convening the session from 14 to 20 November. The difficulty was that a US-Russia summit was to be held 12–13 November at President Bush's private residence in Crawford, Texas. Thus, that option was abandoned.

Hearing that the Arab group planned to object to my proposal, the Latin American and Caribbean group also expressed their concern about the new schedule and requested hat the dates be reconsidered, using the WTO Ministerial Conference as their pretext.

This was a glimpse of the political machinations that go on within the United Nations. I felt as if everyone was testing the resolve of the new President. Discussions within the UN about whether to schedule the General Debate for 10 to 16, 12 to 18, or 14 to 20 November were spinning out of control. There was growing confusion and discord among the Member States.

I believed that if I, the President, did not exercise strong leadership, the carefully achieved consensus would evaporate. I decided I had to push ahead with the original scheduling plan, no matter what. In the end, the original proposal for a seven-day session opening on 10 November with no break over the weekend was adopted. The General Debate would last eight hours each day, and the time allocated for each speech would be 15 minutes.

After the General Debate was successfully scheduled, French Ambassador Jean-David Levitte referred to this as the "Han Formula" and suggested that it be followed every year. Some Member States who appreciated the efficiency of the program also lobbied for its official adoption.

The Mayor of New York City Addresses the UN General Assembly for the First Time

One thing I found shocking upon becoming the President was the poor coordination between the United Nations and New York City. One would imagine that New Yorkers would be proud to host the United Nations and that the relationship between the two would be positive, but that was not the case.

I was surprised to learn that some New Yorkers were strongly predisposed to dislike the United Nations. It is important to note that their criticism of the United Nations was caused less by opposition to the institution itself than by the misbehavior of some diplomats residing in New York, such as diplomats who took advantage of their privileges to repeatedly violate parking regulations and to do so with impunity. The missions of some countries simply refused to pay parking fines. These abuses were regularly taken up in newspaper articles or even on TV news; much media coverage criticized how people associated with the United Nations exploited their special privileges.

In response, the United Nations stressed the tangible and intangible benefits reaped by the city for having the United Nations headquartered there.

Even more surprising was the fact that in the 55-year history of the United Nations, not once had the mayor of New York been invited to address the General Assembly. The first and the last time the New York mayor made an appearance at the General Assembly Hall was when then Mayor Vincent R. Impellitteri (1950–53) was invited to attend the inauguration ceremony of the UN building in 1952. It was understandable why relations between the United Nations and the city had not been the best.

I considered how to improve the awkward relations between the UN and New York City. This was particularly urgent in light of the fact that New York had fallen victim to the recent terrorist attacks. The UN needed to do everything it could to support the people of the city as they struggled to respond to and overcome the tragedy and its aftermath.

As it turned out, the plenary session of the General Assembly, to be held during the week starting October 1, had already been slated to take up the theme of "Measures to Eliminate International Terrorism." I decided to invite Mayor Giuliani, who was striving to secure the relief and recovery of the city, to speak at the General Assembly.

On 26 September, I convened a meeting of the chairs of the regional groupings in the President's Office, where I was able to obtain their consensus on inviting Mayor Giuliani to address the United Nations. Two days later, I consulted with the Mayor, who agreed to speak at the General Assembly Hall on 1 October. This event marked an important and positive milestone in the relations between the UN and New York City.

At 9:30 AM on 1 October, Mayor Giuliani made his appearance in the President's Office behind the podium, after which he delivered a historic speech inside the Assembly Hall. Mayor Giuliani was not a national delegate. Therefore he could not speak at the main session that started at 10:00 AM Instead, arrangements were made for him to speak beginning at 9:45 AM, before the start of the official session.

As expected, Mayor Giuliani's speech received an enthusiastic response. The next day, the morning papers all gave his speech prominent, front-page coverage. The *New York Times* carried a large photograph of Mayor Giuliani speaking as the President, the Secretary-General, and the Under Secretary-General observed from the podium. Mayor Giuliani's speech conveyed to New Yorkers that the United Nations was fighting along with them to overcome the challenges they faced.

When I saw the news coverage, I was pleased that his speech had been realized in this way. I was proud to have been able to contribute in some small way to bridging the divide between the United Nations and New York City.

The benefit of the mayor's speech to the UN was likewise important. Mayor Giuliani assured me of his support to make possible the holding of the General Debate at any time we chose. I felt that this was his gift to the UN in return for the opportunity to address the General Assembly. When he informed me of his support, I was doubly pleased to have invited him to speak.

My office moved immediately to make the most of this opportunity. On 3 October, we issued an official announcement that the General Debate would be held for seven days, from 10 to 16 November.

Order of Speakers Is Based on Position and Rank

At the General Assembly, one of the most challenging tasks, and one requiring meticulous attention, is the order of speakers representing the different countries. Obviously, every government requests what it considers the best dates and times. The order of speeches is particularly difficult in the case of the General Debate, since these are meetings attended by Heads of State and Government.

Most national leaders wish to avoid speaking early on opening day when things are still unsettled, preferring to speak later when things have calmed down and they can receive better attention from the audience. For many years it has been customary for the President of Brazil to deliver the first speech on the opening day of General Debate, followed by the President of the United States, as host country of the United Nations.

The first speech on the opening day overlaps with other events and the mood in the hall tends to be restless and noisy. Also, since the first speech is in the morning, the speaker must prepare early that day, despite the fact that the speech usually does not get much media attention. For these reasons, most countries wish to avoid this time slot.

From the 1st to the 7th annual sessions, the United States delivered the opening speech. Canada was the first speaker for the 8th Session and Chile for the 9th. At the 10th Session of the General Assembly, in 1955, none of the Member States wanted to speak first. In the end, however, Brazil agreed to be the first to address the body. Since then, it has been customary for Brazil to deliver the first speech of the session.

Originally, 31 Heads of State and 19 Heads of Government had been slated to attend the 56th Session of the General Assembly. However, due to the terrorist attacks, many canceled their attendance. The Special Session of the UN General Assembly on Children had also been scheduled to take place from 19 to 21 September, with the attendance of President Nelson Mandela of South Africa and President Kim Dae-jung of the Republic of Korea, among others. This session, however, had to be postponed until May 2002.

In the end, the 56th Session of the General Assembly was attended by 30 Heads of State, 11 prime ministers, one prince, two vice presidents, nine deputy prime ministers serving simultaneously as foreign minister, 96 foreign ministers, one minister of finance, one minister of state, four vice ministers, and 31 ambassadors to the UN. In total, the representatives of 188 of the 189 member nations addressed the General Assembly. In the case of 30 Member States, including the

United States, Brazil, Mexico, South Africa, the Philippines, Pakistan, Venezuela, Kenya, Peru, and Iran, the speeches were delivered by the Heads of State. The government of Iran proposed a "dialogue among civilizations" as a way of easing tension between Islamic and Western cultures and values. His proposal to hold a plenary session just before the General Debate was accepted and, as a result, President Khatami of Iran decided to speak at the session.

On the first day, I made the opening statement before the General Debate and then turned the floor over to Secretary-General Annan. The Secretary-General usually does not speak on these occasions, but for this session, he came down from the podium and delivered a short speech from the speaker's rostrum.

Following the Brazilian President, President Bush spoke. He urged the elimination of international terrorism and also touched on the Palestinian issue. President Bush spoke for 24 minutes. If all the Heads of State and Government exceeded the 15-minute limit, the program would not end on time. President Hugo Ch ávez of Venezuela spoke during the morning session and also went over time. Under the circumstances, I could say nothing. I felt that my hands were tied.

In the year 2000, when I attended the Conference of Presiding Officers of National Parliaments at the United Nations as a representative of the Korean National Assembly, there was an incident in which the microphone had been switched off in the middle of a speech. The first speaker was Mr. Tamisuke Watanuki, Speaker of the Japanese House of Representatives. When his speech continued beyond the time allotted, Ms. Betty Boothroyd, the Speaker of the House of

Commons of the United Kingdom, who was moderating the meeting, without warning turned off the microphone. After that, the other speakers realized they had no choice but to keep to the allotted time. It was particularly interesting to watch Mr. Li Peng, Speaker of China's National People's Congress, leave the rostrum looking quite satisfied with himself at having finished his speech just on time.

At the United Nations, one is treated according to one's status. Heads of State and Government are asked to use a special entrance to the hall. They are escorted to the President's Room behind the podium or to the Secretary-General's waiting room. The Chief of Protocol then escorts the person to the rostrum. In the case of foreign ministers and other members of a delegation, when called to speak they must walk from their seat in the Assembly Hall to take the rostrum.

In the case of a Head of State or Government, the President of the General Assembly will instruct that he or she be escorted into the hall. Heads of State and Government then enter the hall using an entrance obscured by the podium and are asked to take a seat next to the rostrum. Speakers in this category take their place at the rostrum after receiving an introduction and welcome from the President. After they finish speaking, the President and the Secretary-General will descend from the podium and escort the Head of State to the exit of the hall. If it is a Prime Minister, who is not a Head of State, the President and the Secretary-General will not escort him to the exit but will express their appreciation from the podium.

For example, the President will make the following statement to greet President Bush: "The Assembly will hear an address by His Excellency Mr. George W. Bush, President of the

United States of America. I request the Chief of Protocol to escort His Excellency."

After the US President is seated in his chair next to the rostrum, he will say: "On behalf of the General Assembly, I have the honor to welcome to the United Nations His Excellency Mr. George W. Bush, President of the United States of America and to invite him to address the Assembly."

After the speech, President Bush will return to his seat next to the rostrum, and the President of the General Assembly will offer words of appreciation: "On behalf of the General Assembly, I wish to thank the President of the United States of America for the statement just made. May I request the representatives to remain seated while the Secretary-General and I escort His Excellency."

Prime Ministers who are not heads of government will receive the following introduction and be escorted by the Chief of Protocol: "The Assembly will hear the statement by His Excellency Mr. Atal Behari Vajpayee, Prime Minister of India." Such leaders are escorted to the rostrum by the Chief of Protocol and receive the following greeting from the President: "I have the pleasure in welcoming His Excellency Mr. Atal Behari Vajpayee, Prime Minister of India."

After the speech, the President expresses his thanks and asks the Chief of Protocol to escort the leader: "On behalf of the General Assembly, I wish to thank the Prime Minister of India for the statement just made and I request the Chief of Protocol to escort His Excellency."

Protocol becomes less punctilious in the case of foreign ministers and other speakers: "I now give the floor to the Minister of Foreign Affairs of Hungary, His Excellency Mr. Jano Martoniji." The expression of gratitude following the speech is likewise unembellished. "I thank the Minister of Foreign Affairs of Hungary for the statement he has just made."

Through this experience, it was driven home to me that even at the United Nations, whose founding principles are the equality of states and peoples, official treatment is accorded leaders in keeping with their position and rank.

Meeting with President George W. Bush

Of all the speeches by national leaders at the United Nations, the international media give highest priority to addresses by US Presidents. President George W. Bush addressed the General Assembly on the morning of 10 November. I heard that he wished to visit the President of the General Assembly before the speech. The meeting took place in the General Assembly President's Office behind the podium.

It is rare for the President of the United States to pay a visit to a Foreign Minister of any country. In fact, no US President has ever paid a call on Korea's Foreign Minister. Normally, it will be the US Secretary of State who meets with the Foreign Minister, a protocol dictated by their relative positions. However, as the President of the General Assembly I received a visit from the President of the United States.

President Bush arrived, together with his National Security Advisor Condoleezza Rice, his Chief of Staff Andrew Card, and the US Permanent Representative to the United Nations Ambassador John Negroponte. Present on our side were Ambassador Ban Ki-moon, Chef de Cabinet, Ambassador Sun Joon-young, Permanent Representative to the United Nations, and Mr. Oh Joon, Minister-Counsellor at the Office of the President.

President Bush took a seat and began speaking. "President Han seems to have more endurance than most people." When I asked "why," he continued, "If it's only for one or two hours, I can understand, but this year you have to remain seated much longer—four hours in the morning and four in the afternoon. How do you remain seated without using the men's room even once?"

Everyone laughed at his remark. President Bush seems to have a knack for being able to break the ice. He appeared to be aware of the effort to which I had gone to coordinate the schedule of the keynote addresses.

It is true that once you are seated in the President's chair you cannot easily leave it. On the first day of chairing the General Assembly, I ate a heavier breakfast and drank more coffee and water than usual. Midway through the speeches I was possessed of an overwhelming desire to relieve myself and suffered unspeakable discomfort. After that, I abstained from drinking the water placed at my table, merely wetting my lips as necessary.

President Bush's father, former President George H. W. Bush, was visiting Korea on the day of the son's visit to my office. I mentioned that to the President, who replied, "My father was US Ambassador to the UN, but he never invited me to visit the United Nations. Today is my first opportunity to come here." He then continued, saying, "Anyway, in our home, my mother runs things."

In response I said that also in Korea, in good families, it is the mothers who make the major decisions. President Bush looked pleased and said, "I imagine that was the case in President Han's family." His remark made everyone laugh.

Diplomatic relations between the United States and Korea at the time were not particularly good. Korea's policy of reaching out to North Korea disturbed the US. I felt compelled to take this opportunity to explain more about the North Korean nuclear issue and the state of inter-Korean exchanges. "South Korea," I explained, "is not promoting dialogue with North Korea because we trust the North. Rather, we feel we need to engage in a dialogue in order to build mutual trust." I also mentioned that North Korea had recently signed two international treaties on terrorism.

President Bush said it was a good development that North Korea had joined the treaty regimes and expressed his hope for positive results to come from the inter-Korean dialogue.

While I had his attention, I took the opportunity to discuss Korea-US relations: "I am in regular contact with Secretary of State Powell and National Security Advisor Rice to promote further cooperation. I would like to assure you that relations between the two countries will remain strong. I would also like to mention that although Ambassador Negroponte was appointed only recently, he is very much respected by his peers in the United Nations. He has also been offering me full support, and we are in close communication with each other."

President Bush encouraged me to cooperate with Secretary of State Powell and expressed his pleasure at hearing that recently appointed Ambassador Negroponte had already been playing an active role at the United Nations.

That afternoon, Mrs. Kofi Annan organized a party for the spouses of UN ambassadors. At this gathering, Mrs. John

41

Negroponte approached my wife and commented on how happy her husband was that I had praised him in front of President Bush. She went out of her way to express her thanks. When I heard this, I realized that the United Nations is like a small village, where information travels fast.

42

Chapter 3: The Challenge of International Terrorism

The First Resolution of the 56th Session of the General Assembly

The first task I faced after being elected President of the General Assembly was passing a resolution on "Condemnation of terrorist attacks in the United States of America." Because of the September 11 terrorist attacks, the General Assembly had to elect the President a day later than scheduled, an unprecedented event in the history of the United Nations. In this way, the 56th Session of the General Assembly became a historic gathering inextricably linked to the issue of international terrorism. I felt that it was essential that the General Assembly take some kind of action. If the General Assembly had begun on schedule, I knew that some kind of resolution would have already been passed.

A few hours before my election to the presidency, I heard that the Rio Group, comprised of 19 Member States from Latin America, was planning to submit a draft resolution condemning terrorism. If I let them do it, that would lead to multiple drafts being submitted by other groups, which would not only be time-consuming but could lead to a chaotic situation in the General Assembly. I therefore decided to prepare a draft resolution in my capacity as President. I asked Ambassador Ban to gather 20 representatives of the regional groups and draft a resolution on my behalf. The draft of the resolution was finalized after much negotiation among the regional groups just three minutes before the official opening of the 56th Session of the General Assembly.

43

Korean diplomats learned a great deal from the UN diplomacy unfolding with the President's Office at the center. Only 10 years previously, Korea was struggling to become a Member State of the United Nations. These Korean diplomats were witnessing developments and directly participating in efforts that just a few years earlier they could not have imagined.

Neither the Korean diplomats who acted as my aides nor I had had any previous experience conducting negotiations in the United Nations. Nonetheless, we took on the challenges of the task of coordinating the views of the regional groups, with their conflicting interests and opinions. We learned a great deal through this process.

Ambassador Ban showed outstanding ability in coordinating and persuading the Member States regarding the adoption of the resolution. This greatly contributed to a deepening of trust toward Korean diplomats. The representatives of different countries were impressed by his integrity and mediating skills. The favorable reactions he garnered in this way later contributed significantly to the smooth administration of the General Assembly.

At 4:15 PM on 12 September, as I was about to declare the session closed for the day, the representative of Azerbaijan floored a request to make an urgent statement. I decided to grant the request. He said, "Members of the United Nations diplomatic community are not only parking-rules violators; we love this city. We do love New York. We are part of this great city and we want to help it. Therefore, I would like to request that the Secretary-General establish, through the United Nations medical service, a United Nations diplomatic blood-donation center to make our modest contribution to the ongoing New York City rescue process." I requested that the Secretary-General respond. He said he would like to positively consider the proposal. Such was the prevailing mood and sympathy for the people of New York at the United Nations. At the same time, there was tremendous sympathy and support within the international community toward the United States. On that day, the Security Council unanimously adopted a resolution on "Condemnation of terrorist attacks in the United States of America."

Plenary Meeting on "Measures to Eliminate International Terrorism"

I left Seoul on 8 September to be in New York for my inauguration as President of the General Assembly, having been in Seoul for almost two weeks. Because of the terrorist attacks, the United Nations was facing many challenges that required my presence. At the same time, however, I knew there were forces in Korea that opposed my juggling two positions as the Foreign Minister of Korea and the President of the General Assembly, and they would no doubt take advantage of the opportunity to attack me.

Because of this I decided to return to Korea for a brief stay, leaving New York on 25 September. I arrived in Seoul the next day and met with President Kim Dae-jung on 27 September, reporting to him the state of the crisis management at the United Nations General Assembly. On 30 September I was back on a plane to New York to officiate the plenary session on terrorism. While in Seoul, I had responded to various media interviews and expressed my sincere thanks to the people of Korea, the citizens of my hometown, and all those who had extended their support to me.

On 1 October, upon my return to New York, Mayor Giuliani spoke at the opening of the General Assembly in a plenary session being held under the theme "Measures to Eliminate International Terrorism." At the time, Mayor Giuliani was lionized as a hero; thanks to his extraordinary leadership, New York City was gradually returning to normal. Two other heroes, New York City's Police Commissioner and its Fire Commissioner accompanied the mayor on his visit. That day I felt America's true greatness; in time of major crisis the United States creates heroes rather than seeking to blame someone.

The General Assembly session on the eradication of terrorism ended on 5 October, having attracted much international attention, with speakers from 165 Member States. With the exception of the General Debate, never had the General Assembly seen so many national representatives speak. As interest heightened, different Member States started putting forward their various agendas regarding how this plenary session of the General Assembly should end.

On 21 September, British Ambassador to the United Nations and President of the Security Council for the month of September Sir Jeremy Greenstock came to see me. Sir Jeremy stressed the importance of the Security Council and the General Assembly working closely with each other, and that some concrete action on terrorism should result from the plenary session on the eradication of international terrorism.

I also felt that the General Assembly should join the Security Council in adopting a strong resolution to close the plenary session and had discussed this matter several times with Ambassador Ban.

At 4:30 PM on 2 October, I summoned the chairs of the respective regional groups for October, including Sri Lanka, Sudan, the Czech Republic, Ireland, and Haiti. I chose my words carefully as I solicited their views on what would be an appropriate follow-up measure after the conclusion of the plenary session of the General Assembly on the elimination of terrorism.

Haitian Ambassador Pierre Lelong of the Latin American and Caribbean group of 33 countries showed me a copy of a draft prepared by the Rio Group and urged that it be passed by the General Assembly. The African and East European groups endorsed this idea. The Deputy Ambassador of Ireland stated his position that he would support adoption of a resolution as long as it did not invite conflict among Member States.

However, the Ambassador of Sri Lanka then stated that any resolution could be expected to be subject to many different opinions and views and that it might be better simply to issue a President's Statement expressing condolences for the victims, rather than try to pass a resolution.

I was greatly annoyed on hearing this proposal, but controlled my temper. I thought to myself, first the Ambassador of Vietnam, the September chair of the Asian regional group, almost destroys the schedule of the General Assembly, and now the October chair of the Asian group is even worse. In a terse response I said, "I will be sending you the draft of the resolution from the President's Office by 11:00 AM tomorrow. Please try to reach a consensus by 4:00 PM." I then closed the meeting. As planned, the draft was forwarded to the chair of each regional group the following day.

Drafting the Resolution

The following day, 4 October at 12:30 PM, four Ambassadors from the Arab League came to my office with a copy of our draft. I had been expecting the Islamic nations to make some kind of a move.

The group consisted of Ambassador Mikhail Wehbe of the Syrian Arab Republic, Ambassador Abuzed Omar Dorda of the Libyan Arab Jamahiriya, and Tadomori, also of Libya, as well as Ambassador Hussein Hassouna of the Arab League. They contended that the draft was too weak and failed to incorporate language that would differentiate between terrorism and national liberation movements; that was to say, the struggle for Palestinian liberation.

I explained to them that for the resolution to be adopted unanimously by the General Assembly, it must be focused on "common denominators"—those elements acceptable to all the Member States. Under the present circumstances, it is important to focus on basic principles and on demonstrating the political will to confront terrorism. A resolution containing too much specific content or proposing concrete countermeasures would be unlikely to receive the unanimous support of the Member States. I again requested that the four ambassadors try to convince the Arab Member States. However, they were adamant about the need to revise much of the language of the draft.

That evening I invited the chairs of the regional groups to Sichuan Palace, a Chinese restaurant near the UNICEF office. During my presidency, I frequently made use of this restaurant for such meetings. I placed the draft on the table again and asked for their support. This time, the chairperson of the African group voiced his objection, stating that the African nations also felt that the draft seemed watered down: "The Security Council passed a resolution with a much stronger tone, so why is the General Assembly adopting something weaker? Can't you put more meat on it?" Any experienced diplomat would know that a resolution with that kind of tone would never be adopted unanimously by the General Assembly. I sensed that their agenda was either to use the resolution for their political advantage or to simply table it.

I was fuming. I knew that I could not appear weak-kneed in the face of such political maneuverings. If I tried to accommodate everyone's opinion, it would lead to further confusion, and the newly elected President of the General Assembly would not be taken seriously. I was resolved to make my position clear to these national representatives.

In somewhat harsh tones, I said, "If we make the draft stronger, there will be countries that will oppose it. The resolution will not be passed unanimously. You say the draft needs meat and more meat, but if I serve beef, there will be countries that will demand lamb. If I serve lamb, there will be countries that will demand chicken, and others, pork. Under the circumstances, how can we pass a stronger resolution? The Mayor of New York City spoke at the General Assembly for the first time in 55 years. It was unprecedented in the history of the United Nations to have 165 Member States deliver statements on a single agenda item. After having so many speeches delivered over the past five days, if we cannot pass even one resolution, how can the world trust or support the General Assembly? There are voices that call for strengthening and revitalizing the United Nations General Assembly. If we cannot pass a single resolution, after such an important session, it will undermine the credibility and reputation of the General Assembly. Should we not unite and work together to make sure the General Assembly is not seen as weak and useless compared to the Security Council? If we cannot pass even this innocuous and non-confrontational resolution, we might as well abandon the whole idea, as you wish, and release a presidential statement instead. I am asking you to return to your regional groups, speak again with your members, and get them to line up behind this draft."

I was prepared to give up on the resolution, but Ambassador Ban, who was directly involved in its drafting, was immensely disappointed. I sensed that the mood was changing in the United Nations and the international community since the Security Council Resolution was passed on 12 September. In the end, I had to close the General Assembly debate on "Measures to Eliminate International Terrorism" with a presidential statement. I explained this situation in advance to the permanent members of the Security Council and major Member States, including Japan.

Debate on international terrorism dominated the 56th Session of the General Assembly as an issue posing serious challenges to the United Nations. In fact, the issue of international terrorism was originally slated as an agenda item to be addressed by the Sixth Committee, but because of the shock of the terrorist attacks, I used my authority as President to have the issue debated by the entire General Assembly.

Motivated by heightened concern about terrorism, France, Egypt, and others proposed that a foreign minister–level meeting on terrorism be convened at the United Nations. President Khatami of Iran suggested holding a summit on terrorism. Mongolia proposed holding a special session of the United Nations General Assembly on the issue. I believe that by holding sustained debate in the plenary session of the General Assembly on "Measures to Eliminate International Terrorism" the ideas behind these proposals from the Member States were largely accommodated.

Conflicting Definitions of Terrorism

Unfortunately, no resolution was adopted at the end of the plenary session on the elimination of international terrorism, but, on concluding the debate, I issued a statement in which I strongly urged the Member States to take two concrete actions.

There are 12 anti-terrorism conventions to help the international community combat different forms of international terrorism. I urged the Member States to sign and ratify these conventions. I also asked the Member States to support a comprehensive convention on international terrorism and urged that they make every effort to conclude it by 15 November.

Unless otherwise specified, conventions adopted by the United Nations enter into force when two-thirds of the Member States ratify them. Thus far, only the International Convention for the Suppression of Terrorist Bombings has entered into force, leaving another 11 conventions that have yet to enter into force.

Furthermore, I strongly urged that other acts of terrorism not reflected in the 12 existing conventions be included in the comprehensive convention on international terrorism to be drafted by the Sixth Committee. There are dangers involving terrorist attacks using nuclear materials or against nuclear facilities, and I urged that these be addressed.

On 9 October I was once again on a plane to Seoul. Prime Minister Jun'ichiro Koizumi of Japan was scheduled to visit Korea on 15 October. I also had to attend the APEC Ministerial Conference and APEC Summit in Shanghai on 17–20 October. On 23 October I returned to New York. I wished to be present at the UN to celebrate the anniversary of its founding.

United Nations Day commemorates the founding of the UN on 24 October 1945. On this day in 2001, the General Assembly Hall was opened to the UN community and the rostrum was converted to a stage. There was much excitement in the Assembly Hall as singers from India and Pakistan performed. The usual solemn mood of the hall was replaced with a festive one as the families of diplomats sang and danced, forgetting for a moment world conflicts and national differences. Marcel Marceau, the renowned French mime actor, also performed and was greatly appreciated.

UN Day is an unforgettable day for me and for Koreans of my generation. The United Nations brought hope and dreams to young people who struggled in wartime Korea. In fact, the entire population felt a strong debt of gratitude toward the United Nations. I wanted to be at the UN on United Nations Day because the United Nations had played such an important part in my life.

A week after the celebration, I had to return to Seoul to accompany the President to the ASEAN+3 (China, Japan, Korea) Summit in Brunei on 4–6 November.

Chapter 4:
To Reform or Not to Reform
the Security Council

Heated Election Campaign for the Non-permanent Membership of the Security Council

On the morning of 8 October 2001 the mood in the UN General Assembly Hall was tense. The election of the non-permanent members of the Security Council to their two-year terms was to take place that day.

Two days previously, on Saturday, 6 October, my wife and I left the tension that gripped the UN Headquarters behind us and, together with Ambassador Ban and his wife, drove to New Hampshire to take in the beautiful fall colors.

Nestled in the White Mountains of New Hampshire is a historical site that all students of economics and public finance feel compelled to visit at least once in their lifetime. This is the Mount Washington Hotel in Bretton Woods. In the closing days of World War II a historic conference to plan the post-war restructuring of the international economic and financial order was held at this hotel. Ministers of Finance and their advisors and other officials of the United States and the United Kingdom and the Allies participated in this conference, the outcome of which was an agreement to found the International Monetary Fund (IMF) and the International Bank for Reconstruction and Development (IBRD), more commonly known today as the World Bank. The Bretton Woods system was born here.

Hanging on a wall of the Mount Washington Hotel is a photograph of John Maynard Keynes, the economist of *The*

General Theory of Employment, Interest, and Money fame who was one of the British participants in the conference. While not all of Keynes's views were reflected in the final agreement, his contributions had an immeasurable impact on the development of the post-war world economy.

The following day, Sunday, at around 12:30 PM, we were in our car returning to New York, having enjoyed the autumn leaves, when I received a call from the Ministry of Foreign Affairs in Seoul. They had been informed that the United States would attack Afghanistan in an hour.

At 5:15 PM I arrived in New York at the Permanent Mission of the Republic of Korea to the UN and immediately contacted the Foreign Ministry in Seoul to convey my instructions. Due to my absence from Seoul, I had to be especially alert to stay in close contact with my ministry and thus avoid any adverse impact on Korea's diplomatic efforts.

When I assumed the post at the United Nations, I had given assurances that I would effectively initiate timely and appropriate actions in response to any diplomatic crisis that might arise, even if I was absent from the country. For this reason, I felt a particular responsibility to review and assess the situation and give careful thought to developing a response and giving instructions. That night, I did not sleep at all due to a number of telephone conferences with Seoul.

Basing its action on a Security Council resolution (S/RES/1373), the United States decided to attack Afghanistan as retribution against the Taliban government for providing support and haven to al-Qaeda and its leader, Osama bin Laden. Although this was an act authorized by UN Security Council resolutions, this did not diminish the heightened international tension the news produced.

The following day, at 7:40 AM (8:40 PM in Korea), President Bush and President Kim Dae-jung spoke by telephone. President Bush explained the purpose of America's attack on Afghanistan and President Kim expressed his support for this decision. They also agreed that they would continue to exchange views when they next met at the APEC Summit in Shanghai.

On 8 October an election for the rotating five non-permanent members of the Security Council took place. The mood in the United Nations was anxious because this election would lead to the seating of new Security Council members during a time of aggravated international tension.

A vote of two-thirds of the Member States is necessary to elect non-permanent members of the Security Council. Failure to reach this number of votes triggers any of a variety of compromise plans and negotiations within the General Assembly. When that happens, it is not unusual for selection balloting to continue from morning until late at night.

At the 56th Session of the General Assembly, five countries (Bangladesh, Jamaica, Mali, Tunisia, and the Ukraine) were slated for rotation. Candidates from the Asian group were Syria and the United Arab Emirates, while Cameroon and Guinea were candidates from the African group, the Dominican Republic and Mexico were from the Latin American and Caribbean group, and Belarus and Bulgaria were from the East European group.

In the first round of voting, Cameroon, Guinea, Syria and Bulgaria all won seats. Mexico was just two votes short of the 118 votes required for a two-thirds majority but was elected in the second round of voting.

That day, I was scheduled to meet Ambassador John Negroponte for lunch, where we planned to exchange views on

55

Afghanistan. I was concerned that the lunch might be canceled if the elections ran late. Fortunately, the election of the non-permanent Security Council members ended early, and he was able to make it to our luncheon meeting. Ambassador Negroponte seemed quite occupied, and our lunch was interrupted by incessant calls on his mobile phone. Secretary of State Powell was among the callers, and I was able to talk to him.

Secretary Powell and I share a special affinity, since I was the first Foreign Minister of any Member State to meet him after the September 11 terror attacks. I was staying in New York at the time, slated for inauguration as the President, and on 18 September had a meeting with him at the State Department to discuss Korea's future support for the United States. As is customary with the US Secretary of State, Secretary Powell and I held a joint press conference after the meeting. If the counterpart is important enough, the press conference takes place outside the office of the Secretary of State. If not, a simple "door-stepping" interview is held outside the building, after the Secretary of State sees off the other party.

That day, Secretary Powell arranged for a press conference in front of his office. There are foreign ministers or diplomats who prefer to avoid interacting with the press, but I have always seen it as an opportunity. Even if you are thrown challenging questions, with a little wisdom and a sense of humor, it is always possible to come up with a good response. Moreover, one should always take advantage of the interest of American reporters in your story.

In my response to the US media, I wanted to express my sympathy to the American people and the bereaved families of the victims of the September 11 terrorist attacks. I made the following statement to the media:

First of all, I pray for the victims of the terrorist act last week, and also wish to express my condolences to the families and loved ones of the victims. We strongly condemn this heinous act of terrorism and we know that the United States has a great tradition of rallying round the flag in times of crisis. We, the Koreans, are with you in this hour of national distress and anguish and express our strong solidarity with the people and the government of the United States of America. As a strong ally, and in the spirit of the Korea-US Mutual Defense Treaty, Korea will fully cooperate with the United States and will take part in the international coalition in order to support the United States in eradicating the crimes of terrorism. Secretary Powell and I had a very good meeting this morning. I briefed him on the result of the recent South-North ministerial talks. As always, we had a very productive meeting.

The election of the non-permanent members of the Security Council took place inside the General Assembly Hall amidst tensions heightened by international terrorism, and there was concern that the session might become disorderly. In fact, it ended more smoothly than usual, with all ballots cast during the morning session. The staff involved in General Assembly affairs looked happy beyond words. Everyone expressed appreciation, saying that no past election had ended so early. That day, I was treated like an angel who had brought them good luck.

Reforming the Security Council

As the President of the General Assembly, I was required to be directly involved in reform of the United Nations Security Council, a process initiated by General Assembly resolution 48/26 of 3 December 1993. The body responsible for pushing forward reform of the Security Council was officially given the unwieldy name; The Open-ended Working Group on the Question of Equitable Representation on and Increase in the Membership of the Security Council and Other Matters related to the Security Council.

The reform process had been going on for eight years. The President of the General Assembly was automatically asked to serve as the Chairperson for the Working Group on the Reform of the Security Council.

To effectively manage the deliberations of the Working Group, issues were divided into two clusters. Cluster I dealt with issues related to qualifications for representation on the Security Council and the number of Council members. Cluster II included issues related to improving the efficiency of the Council's work.

Cluster I included sensitive issues, such as expanding the membership of the Security Council, the veto, increasing the number of permanent and non-permanent members, and others. Many of these issues were extremely complex and directly involved conflicting national interests of Member States; any consensus was very difficult to reach. In contrast, Cluster II covered issues on which positions were less divisive and, as a result, the discussions had produced considerable progress over the years.

The Security Council is comprised of 15 members. Five countries sit as permanent members, along with 10 non-permanent members. Originally, when the Security Council was established in 1945, it was made up of 11 Member States out of the 45 states that comprised the entire United Nations membership at that time. As former colonies in Africa and elsewhere gained independence, by the early 1960s the number of UN Member States increased to 114. For this reason, on 17

December 1963, at the 18th Session of the General Assembly, the number of non-permanent members was increased from 6 to 10. The United Nations Charter was amended accordingly. Based on this amendment, on 31 August 1965, the UN Security Council was enlarged to 15 members.

The permanent members of the Security Council, as stipulated in the UN Charter, were the victors of World War II: the United States, the United Kingdom, France, Russia (then the USSR), and China. The five permanent members of the Security Council enjoy the privilege of veto power. A negative vote of any of the permanent members will prevent a resolution from being adopted. The non-permanent members are chosen from the five regional groups and are elected for two-year terms.

Renewed debate on the issue of Security Council reform was triggered by the substantial increase in the membership of the United Nations, which by 2001 had grown to 189 Member States. Despite this increase, the membership of the Security Council had remained unchanged since 1965; many voices were raised, urging enlargement of the Council. The key issue was whether to increase the number of permanent members and, if so, whether veto rights would be extended to the new permanent members.

When dealing with issues of this sensitivity, the selection of the officers of the Working Group becomes critical; there was an urgent need to bring together the most competent individuals. Two Vice-Chairpersons were to be appointed for the Working Group. It can be said that the appointment of these positions would determine the success of the group. Since the Vice-Chairperson would chair the group when I was absent, this decision was especially crucial for me.

When dealing with such matters at the United Nations, it is necessary not only to assess individual ability, but also to take into consideration the concerns of the different regional groups. To accomplish anything at the United Nations, a person must have the trust of the regional groups as well as the political ability to convince each government.

The Vice-Chairpersons of the 8th Working Group from the previous year were Ambassador Thornsteinn Ingolfsson of Iceland and Ambassador John de Saram of Sri Lanka. It was agreed that Ambassador Ingolfsson would continue for another year in light of his experience and knowledge, but Ambassador de Saram was not reappointed. He was replaced by Ambassador Mignonette Patricia Durrant of Jamaica, who had consensus support of the regional groups.

Appointing Ambassador Durrant was yet another challenge and was achieved only after a complex and arduous process. The Permanent Mission of Jamaica to the UN had reduced its staffing after the completion of the country's two-year term as non-permanent member of the Security Council in 2001. In addition, Ambassador Durrant had been appointed the Chair of the Preparatory Committee of the Special Session of the United Nations General Assembly on Children that was to open in May and therefore it would be difficult for her to assume a position in the Working Group. I had no choice but to propose Ambassador Muraru Raj Sharma of Nepal. Pakistan, however, objected to this because of its concerns over Nepal's close relations with India. While these discussions continued, I was relieved to hear that Ambassador Durrant had in the end decided to accept the position.

This was a quiet victory for the Coffee Club, a group of middle powers opposed to the expansion of permanent membership of the Security Council, of which Korea is a member. Pakistan is a key player in the Coffee Club and is opposed to India's bid to secure permanent membership. The final appointment in this case, however, was not the result of any behind-the-scenes involvement on my part. Were the President to engage in such maneuvers, he would quickly lose the support of all the Member States. The outcome was merely a coincidence.

The Working Group for UN reform convened its first meeting in my office on 30 January 2002. In view of the critical importance of reforming the Security Council, this group should have been meeting beginning in September of the previous year, immediately after the opening of the General Assembly. However, due to the tight schedule of the first several months of the General Assembly sessions, it had become standard practice to start convening the Working Group after the start of the New Year. The previous year's Working Group had held their first meeting on 5 February 2001.

In February 2002 I convened a meeting to discuss the working procedure for the group. There it was decided to hold five-day sessions in March, May, June, and July; it was also agreed that the Working Group would keep in close communication with the President and key members of the Security Council.

One of the greatest challenges I faced during my presidency was fulfilling my role as the Chairperson of the Working Group for the Reform of the Security Council. Korea was a member of the Coffee Club, which was pushing specific positions with regard to Security Council reform. The President is expected to maintain an even-handed and neutral position. As the Foreign Minister of Korea, I had to speak on behalf of a specific interest group and as the President I was required to be impartial. Clearly, these positions were not mutually exclusive, which was at the root of my difficulty.

To forestall any feeling of mistrust and suspicion among the Member States, I made an official statement declaring my determination to maintain an impartial and neutral position as the President while chairing the Working Group. The Members showed positive understanding toward my position. Even the Permanent Representative of Japan to the UN, Ambassador Yukio Satoh, who was of course keen to see an expansion of permanent membership of the Security Council, not only showed understanding but also extended his support.

On 31 January, at 9:30 AM, I invited the ambassadors of the five permanent members of the Security Council to my office to plumb their thoughts. In organizing the Working Group deliberations, I planned to touch on such issues as the working method of the Security Council, its decision-making processes, including the veto, and finally, the question of increasing the membership of the Security Council.

In response to this, Ambassador Sergey Lavrov of the Russian Federation suggested that the Working Group should first address the issue of how to increase the membership of the Security Council. The previous year's Working Group had begun with the issue of the Council's decision-making processes; this had led to deadlock when the debate turned to whether new permanent members should have veto power. As a result, the deliberations saw no progress. Based on this experience, I proposed that we should begin with issues that would be easiest to deal with. I also suggested that we invite the former, the present, and the next president of the Security Council to be present at the first session of the Working Group.

The next meeting of the Working Group took place at 10 AM on 11 March in the Chamber of the Trusteeship Council. Out of the six major organs established by the Charter, the work of the Trusteeship Council had been reduced the most substantially. When the United Nations was founded, there were many trust territories, but, with the independence of Palau in 1994, they had all gained their independence.

Because there was little for the Trusteeship Council to do, at an official meeting of heads of major organs of the United Nations on 30 October 2001, the President of the Trusteeship Council suggested the dissolution of the Council. The Trusteeship Council chamber was located to the right of the Office of the President, and I thought the room would be convenient for our use.

The first session of the Working Group, which discussed enlargement of the Security Council, began with heated arguments between members representing conflicting positions. Japan and Germany, as states aspiring to gain permanent status, and India, Brazil, and South Africa, also wishing to join the permanent membership, felt that enough discussion had taken place and it was time for negotiations to begin. The G-10, a group that included Australia and Belgium, supported this view. The Working Group had been meeting for nine years, and members evinced a feeling of frustration and disappointment, especially among the countries aspiring to permanent membership.

There was strong opposition to this from the Coffee Club, comprised of states with no realistic chance of becoming permanent members on the Council. Opposition from Italy was much stronger than I had expected. The meeting always came to an impasse and nothing could be decided.

63

There are three important issues that drive Security Council reform. The first issue relates to the ratio of members to Security Council membership. In 1965, when the Security Council was enlarged to 15 members, there were 114 Member States in the United Nations. The ratio of Security Council membership was 7.7:1, or 13 percent. Even though the number of Member States increased to 189 by 2001, the number of members in the Security Council remained unchanged. Today the ratio comes to only 12.6:1, or 8 percent. For the Security Council to maintain the same ratio it had in 1965, it would need to be enlarged to 24 members. This is one of the underlying issues driving the reform of the Security Council.

Second, over the years, the nations defeated in World War II, specifically Japan and Germany, have expanded their power and influence. These two countries' contributions to the UN budget are second only to that of the United States. In the year 2002, the United States ranked first in assessed contributions to the UN budget, at 22 percent of the total; Japan ranked second at 19.669 percent; and Germany third with 9.845 percent. The latter two countries' contributions to the UN budget far exceeded those of the remaining permanent members of the Security Council combined. Thus, they have been demanding status that corresponds to their acceptance of responsibility within the international community. This is another factor leading to the discussion of Security Council reform.

The third issue driving reform is demand for increased transparency and democratic administration of the Security Council. Especially among the nonaligned countries, there are many voices calling for democratization of the decision-making process in the Security Council. Since the end of the Cold War, Member States have become increasingly concerned about the nature and role of the Security Council. Much public opinion is critical of the veto and other practices of the Security Council that are considered undemocratic.

For this reason, many Member States supported the idea of enlarging the membership of the Security Council. Opinions, however, were divided among the Member States when it came to such issues as the specific number of members on the Security Council, whether the number of permanent members should be increased and, if so, by how many and whether the veto should be extended to the new permanent members.

With regard to the reform of the Security Council, the United Nations membership can be divided into four groups. The first group would be the current five permanent members of the Security Council. The second group would be the non-aligned countries. The third group would include so-called aspirants, such as Japan and Germany, seeking a permanent place on the Security Council. There are also developing nations, such as India, Brazil, and South Africa, looking for permanent seats; these countries have been referred to as "pretenders." The fourth group is the Coffee Club—some 30 countries, including Italy, Spain, Mexico, Argentina, Korea, and Egypt, who oppose increasing the number of permanent members on the Security Council.

Regarding the enlargement of the Security Council, opinions were divided between a new total between 20 and 26 members, with a majority of the Member States opting for a

Security Council membership of 24, an increase of nine seats over the current membership. Russia claimed that 21 would be an optimal number from the standpoint of efficiency, while the UK, France, Japan, and Germany felt that 24 would be more realistic. The nonaligned countries preferred 26.

The United States at first refused to compromise its position that it would be unrealistic to have more than 21 seats on the Security Council, but by April 2000 it had changed its stance. In return for acceptance of a proposal to reduce its assessed contribution from 25 percent in 2000 to 22 percent of the UN regular budget, the United States modified its position and agreed to a slight increase over 21 members. Together with the US contribution being lowered, Japan's contribution was also reduced slightly, from 20.573 percent to 19.669 percent.

As for expansion of the permanent membership of the Security Council, two proposals seemed to represent the mainstream: 2+3 or 2+3PRRS, where PRRS stands for Permanent Regional Rotating Seats. In the 2+3 option, together with Japan and Germany, three additional permanent members would be elected each from the Asian, African, and Latin American and Caribbean regional groups. In the 2+3PRRS option, along with Japan and Germany there would be three rotating seats elected from developing states. Each regional group is given the freedom to determine the rotation of the candidate to be elected. However, these options were not necessarily supported by all the Member States.

The Coffee Club, for one, did not support either plan. They asserted that rotating permanent seats in the Security Council should be applied not only to the developing nations but to the developed nations as well. On the other hand, the Arab nations were insistent upon securing one permanent seat in the Security Council because they comprised 12 percent of the Member States. Thus, the conflicting claims and interests of Member States varied widely.

The United States and Russia preferred a limited increase in the number of new permanent seats. The United Kingdom, France, Japan, and Germany proposed an increase of five permanent seats and four non-permanent seats. The majority of Member States wanted a total increase of about 10 new seats, including both permanent and non-permanent members.

The difficulty in expanding the Security Council lies in the fact that the candidates for new permanent seats are limited to countries like Japan, Germany, India, Brazil, and South Africa. A system that offers special privileges to a select group of countries will naturally not be well received by the rest of the Member States. For this reason, a majority of middle powers that are actively contributing to the work of the UN are concerned that a new system would lead to their marginalization. Many of the nonaligned nations proposed that if there is no agreement on enlargement of the permanent membership, for the time being there should be enlargement of only the non-permanent membership. The Coffee Club endorsed this idea.

Another key issue debated as part of Security Council reform was the veto. The current permanent members of the Council demanded that the veto be maintained in its present form. Japan and Germany, based on the principle of the sovereign equality of all Member States of the United Nations spelled out in the UN Charter, demanded that the new permanent members be given equal veto rights. In a worst-case scenario, however, they seemed to be willing to waive the veto. At the same time, developing nations demanded that the veto be extended to any new permanent member representing developing nations.

Related to this debate issue was the question of curtailing the use of the veto. In recent years, the functioning of the Security Council has been considerably strengthened as a result of the permanent members' self-imposed restraint on their exercise of the veto. When members have resorted to the veto without restraint, the Council has been paralyzed. To avoid this, the permanent members have been exercising restraint in applying the veto in recent years.

There was widespread consensus among the Member States that the use of the veto by the permanent members should be curtailed. However, the current five permanent members refused to consider any formal modification and took a firm stance that the veto should be maintained in its present form. The nonaligned nations, aiming toward eventual abolition of the veto, made their position clear that the veto should be restricted to "enforcement measures" as stipulated in Chapter VII of the UN Charter. In January 2002 France made clear its willingness to consider proposals to formalize voluntary restraint on use of the veto in the Security Council.

Issues related to the number of new permanent members and the veto were part of the Cluster I agenda. In Cluster II, the need to enhance the efficiency and working methods of the Security Council were the key agenda items. It was not difficult to gain consensus on these issues.

UN reform cannot be discussed isolated from the question of amending the UN Charter. The procedure for minor changes is governed by Article 108 of the Charter, in which amendments must be adopted by a vote of two-thirds of the UN membership and enter into force when ratified by two-thirds of the Member States, including all five of the permanent members of the

Security Council. Major substantive amendments must be adopted by a vote of two-thirds of the Members, including nine members of the Security Council; a General Assembly session for amendment of the Charter must be convened. An amendment will enter into force when adopted by a vote of two-thirds of the Members of that General Assembly and ratified by two-thirds of the Members of the United Nations, including the permanent members of the Security Council.

In November 1998 the 53rd Session of the General Assembly adopted the following Resolution (A/RES/53/30) on Security Council reform:

> Mindful of Chapter XVIII of the Charter of the United Nations and of the importance of reaching general agreement as referred to in resolution 48/26 of 3 December 1993, the General Assembly determines not to adopt any resolution or decision on the question of equitable representation on and increase in the membership of the Security Council and related matters, without the affirmative vote of at least two thirds of the Members of the General Assembly.

This resolution was introduced by the members of the Coffee Club. It states that an affirmative vote of *at least two thirds* is necessary for reform, meaning that Security Council reform will require the support of a minimum of two-thirds of the Members of the General Assembly. Germany's interpretation was that a two-thirds vote would be sufficient, but the Coffee Club states disagreed and argued against this view. This is one more case of the intensity of the political and diplomatic maneuverings within the United Nations.

Security Council reform involves problems of not only a substantive but also of a procedural nature. For this reason, these issues had remained unresolved even after eight years of debate, with the work passed on to successive sessions of the General Assembly. This task was similarly carried over to the 56th Session of the General Assembly, where the responsibility for it fell to me.

The Working Group on Security Council Reform

Under my chairmanship, the group held four sessions: the first session, 31 January 2002; the second session, 11–15 March 2002; the third session, 13–17 May 2002; and the fourth and final session, 10–13 June 2002.

The second session was held on 11 March from 10 AM in the Trusteeship Council chamber and was attended by 80 or so countries. In this session, 22 Member States delivered addresses. However, positions were deeply divided and the session made no real progress. My impression was that the possibility of reaching a dramatic breakthrough was bleak. Moreover, the Members' sense of fatigue from the prolonged process of reform debate was stronger than I had thought.

There were, however, some differences in the debates at this year's Working Group. The level of interest among the Security Council members was exceptionally high. During the third session, which began on 13 May, the ambassadors of all 15 members of the Security Council were present, as were representatives of some 60 nations. Speeches were delivered by eight members of the Security Council, including Ambassador Ole Peter Kolby of Norway, the President of the Security Council for the month of March, and the permanent representatives of the United Kingdom, France, and Singapore. Nine members of the Working Group, including Japan, Germany,

Italy, and Argentina, made statements during the session. There had never been such active debate and vigorous exchange among members of the General Assembly and the Security Council. I was told that in the Working Group of the previous year only three members of the Security Council attended the sessions.

Japan was particularly involved in these sessions and worked actively to promote its national interests. Ambassador Motohide Yoshikawa, the Deputy Permanent Representative of Japan assigned to the Security Council, and the political affairs specialists were not only proficient in English but also in other languages. They made great efforts to develop consensus among the Member States. Japan even led the debate during the session on the issue of the veto.

Indeed, Japan seemed determined to make January 2004 the tenth anniversary of the Working Group of the Security Council reform, a turning point in pushing forward the reform of the Council. It was only natural that Japan should be so actively involved. At the time there was a strong sense that there would be an enlargement of the permanent membership of the Security Council and that when that happened Japan would secure a permanent seat. The question seemed to be more one of timing and content of the reform package. It should be understood that a substantial amount of effort and energy must go into political and diplomatic maneuverings for a country to achieve such a result.

Although Germany also aspired to a permanent seat on the Security Council, German diplomats seemed passive compared to those from Japan. Perhaps Germany's focus at that time was more on its position within the EU and the

Kosovo issue. In any event, Germany did not actively involve itself in discussions on the question of enlarging the Security Council.

In contrast to Japan and Germany, Italy had no realistic possibility of securing a place on the Council. Its response was to oppose any enlargement of the permanent membership of the Security Council. Italy, a member of the Group of Eight, like Japan and Germany, was among the defeated countries in World War II. Spain voiced its support for Italy's position. The statement made by Counsellor Ana María Menéndez of the Spanish Mission in charge of Security Council reform was very convincing. She said that in the process of European integration, Italy and Spain were accorded equal treatment to Germany. Why, then, should Germany be given special treatment in the international community? One could sense Spain and Italy's emotional reaction and opposition as a testament to their refusal to accept such discriminatory treatment.

The fourth and final session of the Working Group took place beginning at 10 AM on 10 June. Since this was to be the last session of the Working Group for the 56th Session of the General Assembly, there was some apprehension in the room. A statement from the Italian representative triggered a debate of unprecedented acrimony. Italy's statement was as follows:

> Since no agreement has been reached on an enlargement of other categories of membership, after nine years of debate, priority consideration for the time being should be given to an enlargement of non-permanent membership only.

Japan immediately expressed its opposition to this proposal and was supported by the United Kingdom, Germany, and India. On the other side, Spain, Argentina, Pakistan, and Korea expressed their support for Italy's proposal. The meeting grew rancorous as the two blocs refused to budge from their positions.

I could not understand why Italy had made this proposal at this particular time. Perhaps the Italians wanted to take advantage of the fact that the Foreign Minister of Korea, a member of the Coffee Club, was chairing the Working Group, and may have wanted to leverage that presumed advantage.

From the outset, however, I had made clear my position that I would not side with any specific state or group of states. Regardless of what my country's position was, I was resolved to remain strictly impartial, taking an international stance as the President of the General Assembly.

Acknowledging the impasse in the deliberations, I had to announce, "Many views were recorded during the sessions. We will continue to discuss these issues in ensuing informal deliberations." With these words, I closed the last session of the Working Group. This was the best decision I could make at that time and I had to leave the unresolved issues to the President of the 57th Session of the United Nations General Assembly.

Chapter 5: Tensions Between the Offices of President and Secretary-General

The Size and Functions of the Office of the President

The UN Secretariat allocated only four staff personnel to the Office of the President of the General Assembly: two secretaries, one security person, and a driver and car for the President's exclusive use. Presidents of the General Assembly may, however, bring diplomats and staff from their own country to support their work. Since 1988, the Office of the President has been allocated annual funds of $250,000 to cover activities and operating expenses. Most of this amount was spent in hiring additional staff, travel expenses for staff, and the Office's operating costs. In addition to this, the President's personal budget for the 56th Session of the General Assembly was $181,628, which covered expenses for overseas travel, expenses while in New York, etc.

A capable Chef de Cabinet is essential to the successful running of the Office. Since I also held the post of Foreign Minister, I would be obliged to be away from New York often and my Chef de Cabinet would have to play an important role, managing the Office during my absence. Fortunately, Ambassador Ban Ki-moon had recently transitioned from his position as Vice Foreign Minister to that of a resident Ambassador at the Institute of Foreign Affairs and National Security.

Although a former Vice Minister is overqualified for the position of the Chef de Cabinet, I decided to ask Ambassador

Ban to undertake this role. In the spirit of public service, he willingly accepted my invitation. I perceived in his resolve a sense of mission as a diplomat representing Korea and an earnest wish to help me succeed as the first Korean to serve as President of the United Nations General Assembly. We have long been associated in the pursuit of Korea's foreign policy. When I was appointed Korean Ambassador to the United States in April 1993, Ambassador Ban was the Deputy Chief of Mission at the Korean Embassy in Washington. We worked very closely together to coordinate our policy with that of the United States in dealing with the first North Korean nuclear crisis. The outcome of our cooperation with the United States in dealing with North Korean nuclear development was the Geneva Agreed Framework of October 1994. I knew from those days that he was a man of integrity and self-sacrifice for the sake of the public good.

I entrusted Ban with all personnel decisions. He selected six brilliant diplomats from the Foreign Ministry to work with us in the General Assembly, including Mr. Oh Joon (currently Korea's Deputy Ambassador at the Korean Mission to the United Nations) as Minister-Counsellor for Political Affairs, Mr. Moon Ha-young (currently Korean Ambassador in Uzbekistan) as Minister-Counsellor for Economics Affairs, Mr. Kim Bong-hyun (currently Director-General for Consulate Affairs in Seoul) as Special Assistant, and Mr. Yoon Yeo-chul (currently Special Assistant to the Secretary-General) as my secretary. In addition, the Korean Mission to the United Nations supported us by dispatching Mr. Choi Seok-young, Counsellor (currently Minister for Economic Affairs at the Korean Embassy in Washington), Mr. Choi Jong-hyun, Counsellor (Ministry of Foreign Affairs and Trade), and Mr.

Lee Baek-soon, First Secretary (currently Counsellor at the Korean Embassy in Washington). They all worked very hard and did their best in making the Korean presidency at the United Nations General Assembly a success, leaving a lasting impression on all the members of the United Nations.

Ambassador Ban arrived in New York on 20 June 2001, approximately three months before I was to be inaugurated, to take over affairs from his predecessor and make preparations for the transition. To our surprise, no administrative handover procedure existed in the Office of the President of the General Assembly. Even more astonishing was that in the 55-year history of the UN General Assembly, the Office had kept no institutional records of proceedings, activities, or handovers.

Over its history, the General Assembly must have debated many crucial issues, including world peace, the elimination of poverty, economic development and growth, human rights, and many others. A Millennium Summit had even been convened in the year 2000, and yet there were no institutional records of either regular or special sessions of the General Assembly, nor of any of the previous year's session.

From the 56th Session of the General Assembly, I had all activities of the Office of the President archived and passed on to the next President. I considered this important to ensure continuity and consistency in the management of the President's Office, for the sake of the United Nations.

War of Nerves Over Protocol

Unseen tensions and rivalry, as well as cooperation, mark relations between the Office of the President of the General Assembly and the Executive Office of the Secretary-General. The conflicts between the two offices during the 46th Session of the General Assembly (1991–92) were in some ways extreme, but in other ways representative. Perhaps the Secretary-General wished to assert his authority over the President by removing his office from the 38th floor. The UN Charter does not stipulate which title is superior.

The former Secretary-General's actions may have been exceptional, but it would be untruthful to deny the consistent presence of unseen frictions and tensions and a kind of tug-of-war between the two offices. The President of the General Assembly takes pride in representing the "world's parliament" of Member States that is the General Assembly. The President does not need the Secretary-General's approval, but the Secretary-General's inauguration requires the General Assembly's approval and the incumbent must take an oath before the President.

On the other hand, the Secretary-General serves for a five-year term and has a seat on and a voice in the deliberations of the Security Council, in which the President is unable to participate. The Secretary-General has a sense of being directly involved in efforts to resolve international disputes and lay the foundation for world peace. The Secretary-General also exercises authority over UN personnel and budget decisions. The Secretary-General thus can take pride in representing and running the UN both in name and in fact.

Tensions often surface during international conferences organized by the UN. Since these meetings are organized by the Secretariat, the staff naturally give the Secretary-General priority. The Office of the President finds this annoying and demands that the President be accorded precedence over the Secretary-General at meetings attended by both.

For this reason, the offices have often waged a war of nerves over the order of speeches, movement, seating, and other protocol issues at international conferences. The 56th session of the General Assembly was not exempt from such protocol conflicts, but this does not mean that there was any personal animosity between Secretary-General Annan and me when I served as President of the General Assembly.

While struggling with the gap between the ideal and the reality, the UN remains the only world body at the disposal of diplomats from around the world to gather and work for world peace, development, and other common goals. We should not imagine it as an ideal world removed from reality, but instead as a forum embodying the shared pains and sufferings of humanity.

Accepting to Have Annan Deliver the Nobel Lecture

The Nobel Peace Prize was created in 1901 and, thus, the year 2001 marked its centennial. In this significant year, the Norwegian Nobel Committee decided to award the Nobel Peace Prize to the United Nations and its Secretary-General Kofi Annan. I received word of the decision just prior to the official announcement, while I was in Seoul, where I had gone to report on my activities. I was informed from the start that the prize would be awarded to the Secretary-General alone. It turned out, however, that the Norwegian Nobel Committee decided to give half of the prize to the United Nations organization as a whole and the other half to Secretary-General Annan, individually.

At 10:30 PM on 11 October, I called Ambassador Ban to ask him to convey my congratulations to Secretary-General Annan. It was 9:30 AM on 11 October New York time, and the Secretary-General had just arrived at the reception venue at the UN. Ban handed his phone to Annan, to whom I said, "I

79

extend my heartfelt congratulations on your receipt of the Nobel Peace Prize. No one is more worthy of this honor than you. My wife sends her warmest congratulations to you and Nane."

I asked Ban to organize, in the name of the President of the General Assembly, an official reception for celebration. The following day, the Secretary-General was invited to a celebratory event in the General Assembly Hall. I was told that when he entered the hall, representatives of all the Member States greeted him with a standing ovation. The acting President of the General Assembly read my message, and the chairs of the five regional groups each paid tribute on the conferral of the award.

I was contacted by Annan when I returned to work in New York on 23 October. He said that he would accept the Peace Prize awarded to him, but that he would like me to go to Oslo to receive that part of the Nobel Peace Prize conferred upon the United Nations as a whole. He wanted me to attend the award ceremony with him. Until that moment, I had not expected that I should receive the prize on behalf of the United Nations. I felt, however, that this was something that should not be decided by the Secretary-General alone and at his sole discretion. Rather, the decision required an organization-wide consensus within the UN; it would be problematic if it were decided informally on an individual basis between the Secretary-General and the President.

I asked to convene an official meeting of the representatives of the six principal organs of the United Nations, as set out in the UN Charter. The six of us, the Secretary-General, the President of the Security Council, the President of the Economic and Social Council, the President of the Trusteeship

Council, the President of the International Court of Justice, and myself, met in the Office of the Secretary-General at 11:30 AM on 30 October. Secretary-General Annan asked each participant who they thought should receive the Nobel Peace Prize on behalf of the UN. They all replied that the President of the General Assembly was the sole representative of the United Nations and therefore should go to Oslo to accept it. In this way it was determined that I would travel to Oslo to receive the award on behalf of the United Nations.

As the Nobel Peace Prize was to be awarded to the United Nations as a whole, I asked to be accompanied not only by the staff at the UN headquarters, but also by representatives of the UN staff in the field, who were dispatched to all corners of the world. Previous to that occasion, the Nobel Peace Prize had been awarded to four UN-related bodies: the Office of the United Nations High Commissioner for Refugees in 1954 and 1981, the United Nations Children's Fund in 1965, the International Labor Organization in 1969, and the UN Peacekeeping Force in 1988.

The Nobel Peace Prize Award Ceremony was held, as always, in Oslo, Norway, on 10 December, the date of Alfred Nobel's death. On 9 December, there was a press conference and a rehearsal at the City Hall, followed in the evening by a "little dinner" on the eighth floor of the Grand Hotel for the awardees, their spouses, the Norwegian Nobel Committee members, and its secretary.

The dinner started at 7:00 PM It was indeed a little dinner with only 10 of us attending, including Secretary-General and Mrs. Annan, my wife, and myself. Annan urged me to express our gratitude at the beginning. I began my greeting as follows: "I want to thank you for holding this dinner for us the night before the great award ceremony tomorrow. I am especially honored by this 'little dinner' at the Grand Hotel." People burst into laughter at this joke. They all found the idea of a little dinner at a "grand hotel" amusing. We were told that major political figures insisted upon being invited to this dinner many times in the past, but were always rejected. The little dinner continued to remain unknown to most people in Oslo.

The following day, Secretary-General Annan and I left the hotel at 12:52 PM, arriving at the City Hall only six minutes later. The Norwegian Nobel Committee members were lined up at the front gate; with a fanfare the gate opened and we were led in.

After the arrival of the King and the royal family and a brief pre-event serenade, the ceremony began with the Norwegian Nobel Committee Chair's opening address, which lasted for about 20 minutes. When he finished his speech, he announced, "Now we will present the Nobel Peace Prize Medal and Diploma to Korean Foreign Minister Han Seung-soo, representing the United Nations." I did not expect him to refer to me as the Korean Foreign Minister instead of as the President of the United Nations General Assembly. He had repeatedly confirmed with me the pronunciation of my name prior to the ceremony and he did well with it during the actual event. I greeted the audience, holding the Medal in my right hand and the Diploma in my left hand. Secretary-General Annan, who received the prize after me, stood beside me in the same pose, holding up the Medal and the Diploma.

After the award ceremony, together we visited the Royal Palace. His Majesty King Harald V and members of the royal family, who had attended the award ceremony in the City Hall, were waiting for us. The Queen, who was not able to attend the ceremony because of a leg injury, was also there to greet us. The four of us had a private meeting with the King and the Queen in their private lounge and then moved on to the reception.

The Nobel Peace Prize dinner and banquet began at 7:30 PM Approximately 250 national and international dignitaries were invited to the dinner at the Grand Hotel. At the end of the dinner, Annan asked me to go first in making a thank-you speech.

I began my greetings by saying, "Chairman Berge of the Norwegian Nobel Committee, the members and secretary of the Norwegian Nobel Committee, President Kufuor of Ghana, Prime Minister Bondevik, President of the Parliament, Chief Justice of the Supreme Court, the Nobel Peace Prize Laureates, excellencies, distinguished guests, members of the UN staff who have joined us from far corners of the world, and members of our two families, ladies and gentlemen, As the President of the UN General Assembly and Korea's Foreign Minister, as well as a Member of the Korean National Assembly, I have had many opportunities to give speeches in different places, but never before have I had to go over such a long list of hosts and guests before I could even begin." The entire room roared with laughter. Everyone later commented that my speech was the highlight of the gala dinner. Annan stood up after my speech. He paid respect to me by saying, "President Han Seung-soo has said everything I wanted to say. The only thing left for me to do is to propose a toast."

Frankly speaking, I had not been in a good mood all day, feeling that I had been forced to play second fiddle to Annan during the award ceremony. It was due above all to the fact that I had let him deliver the acceptance speech alone. The

83

Norwegian Nobel Committee had informed us of the time constraints but had left it up to us whether he would be the sole speaker or we would both speak. Twice in New York, Annan had asked me what I thought about him being the only speaker, which was clearly his preference. I agreed to his solo speaking because the Secretary-General himself was indisputably the laureate, and I was certain that he would speak about the ideals of the UN in his address. Once at the award ceremony, however, I regretted having given up the opportunity because I did not feel he had adequately covered the ideals and the role of the United Nations. I thought I could have filled in the gap that he had left out. There is a Korean proverb "playing the role of a chicken instead of a pheasant," which was exactly how I felt that day.

Nonetheless, Annan and I deepened our mutual respect through the occasion of receiving the Nobel Peace Prize together. During dinner, we discussed peace and the eradication of poverty, affirming our conviction of sharing the same mission. We promised to work together more closely in the fight against poverty and disease in Africa and to unite our efforts toward the improved well-being of humanity and global peace.

Annan has a reputation for rarely giving free expression to feelings of joy and pleasure. He is known for being careful and cautious in all things, avoiding close relationships. He is also known as a family person who avoids dining out as much as possible. On that day, I felt that he was opening his mind to me.

The dinner reception continued until 11:00 PM, followed by a ball. As I was scheduled to depart at 5:00 AM the next morning, I had to leave the venue early. Several weeks before the announcement of the Nobel Peace Prize, I had accepted an invitation from Mr. Ruud Lubbers, UN High Commissioner for Refugees, to speak on 12 December at the 50th anniversary of its Office in Geneva. To keep the promise, I had to forego the golden opportunity of attending the royal gala dinner given in Stockholm for all the Nobel laureates by the King and Queen of Sweden on the evening of 12 December 2001. I was sad that my wife and I had to miss it. I was even sadder that not a single Korean media person had been present at the ceremony to cover the historic awarding of the centennial Nobel Peace Prize

Japan at the International Conference on Financing for Development

The Summit segment of the International Conference on Financing for Development was held on 18–22 March 2002 in Monterrey, Mexico.

President Vicente Fox of Mexico made an opening statement at 9:00 AM on 18 March, followed by speeches by Secretary-General Annan and myself. The Office of the President of the General Assembly insisted that the President go first, but the UN Secretariat refused to change the order. The Office explicitly expressed its discontent, but the Secretariat did not respond.

In my statement, I urged developing countries to focus on training talented people, promoting sound macroeconomic policies, and eliminating corruption. I emphasized the importance of building intangible infrastructure, such as the rule of law. I also pointed out that foreign direct investment and export earnings were the most effective source of financing. I called on rich, developed countries to open and expand their markets for the products of developing countries and to adopt growth-stimulating policies to encourage domestic consumer spending.

My speech was followed by speeches from the President of the World Bank, the Managing Director of the International Monetary Fund, and the Director-General of the World Trade Organization. The leaders of various states spoke after them, beginning with Venezuelan President Chávez, representing the Group of 77 and China. The Group of 77 was named after 77 developing countries that signed the Joint Declaration at the end of the first session of the UN Conference on Trade and Development (UNCTAD) in 1964. Based on the Charter of Algiers, it is now the largest caucus group in the UN General Assembly, with a membership of more than 130 countries.

At their request, the Group of 77's representative has always come last in the order of speeches, but at the International Conference on Financing for Development, because the meeting was for the benefit of states struggling with poverty, their speaker went first. President Chávez had a reputation for always addressing the General Assembly far longer than the time allotted to him. This day was no exception, and he went on at length, exceeding the original time limit of five minutes and not ending even after 10 minutes. President Fox, who was acting as moderator, finally rang the warning bell to have Chávez bring his remarks to a close, but Chávez continued, retorting and expressing his outrage that more than five minutes were given to the leaders of world organizations and that the leader of a sovereign state was not allowed to speak for more than five minutes.

The second speaker was Prime Minister José María Aznar of Spain, the chair of the European Union. All the subsequent leaders of states spoke longer than the five minutes given to them. The surprising exception was President Fidel Castro of Cuba, famous for his long speeches. Once his five minutes had expired, he suddenly took a note from his pocket and read from it: "A special situation created by my participation in this Summit obligates me to immediately return to my country. The leader of the Cuban delegation will then be Comrade Ricardo Alarcón de Quesada, Speaker of the National Assembly of People's Power. I entrust him with the prerogatives corresponding to me as a Head of State attending this conference." With that, he walked out, leaving everyone taken aback. It later came to light that his exit had been cleverly arranged by the host country, Mexico, which was anxious to avoid a direct meeting between President Castro and US President Bush.

The conference received extensive media coverage in the United States and Europe, but media participation from Asian countries was more limited than had been expected. Japan had dispatched to the conference only its Senior Vice-Minister of Foreign Affairs. The vice-minister had to endure a cold reception, although from a protocol perspective this was inevitable. A vice-minister ends up being the lowest-ranking representative at an international conference attended by national leaders and cabinet ministers.

Speeches by heads of state and government, of however small a country, are given priority at international conferences. Prime ministers who are not heads of government and cabinet members come next. In order of protocol, a vice-minister's statement is put far down, at the end of the line. As a conference winds up, most of the leaders and ministers, having completed their speeches, will start returning to their home countries. Alternatively, they may leave the venue for bilateral talks with other leaders. As a result, the Japanese vice-minister was forced to give his statement in the late afternoon on the last day to a vast and almost empty hall. This was unfortunate because Japan is one of the world's most generous providers of development aid. It could have been a great opportunity for Japan, aspiring to a permanent seat on the Security Council, to garner the support of the leaders of developing countries attending the conference.

In contrast, Romano Prodi, President of the European Commission, stressed solidarity between Africa and the EU, and was treated to warm applause from the audience, the first applause for any speaker at the Conference. Witnessing this, I clearly sensed the strong determination for development among Africa's developing countries. This made it all the more painful to see Asian countries, many of which have only recently emerged from poverty, ignoring Africa's earnest desire for development.

The World Assembly on Ageing in Madrid

The Second World Assembly on Ageing opened in Madrid, Spain, on 8 April 2002. Here also, at this UN-organized meeting, the Secretary-General preceded me in speaking. Princess Christina delivered a welcoming speech. She was nine months pregnant at the time, and in her discomfort one could sense her strong commitment to the success of the conference.

After her welcome, Secretary-General Annan made an opening speech. When he stated, "I am sixty-four years old today, making me a most qualified participant in the World ssembly on Ageing," someone shouted out "Happy birthday!" ending the entire audience into laughter. My turn came after he Secretary-General. I said:

> The world has an additional one million aged population every month. No measures are taken regarding the problems of these people, particularly on the part of developing countries. The entire world should make concerted efforts about it, along with issues of the environment and poverty. The experience, knowledge, and technology of knowledge-based societies tackling the aging issue can be utilized in developing countries. I urge that the international plan of action to be adopted at this conference be powerfully implemented.

Spain's Prime Minister Aznar gave a luncheon for ecretary-General Annan and me at the Prime Minister's official residence. On the table was a birthday cake with 64 candles for Annan. The Prime Minister gave Annan a red bullighter's cape as a gift. The Secretary-General draped the cape ver his shoulders like a bullfighter as he left the building, parking applause and laughter.

The aging of society is an extremely difficult challenge or developed as well as for developing countries. Regrettably, this conference drew very little international attention. The conference was overshadowed by the Middle ast Peace Conference being held simultaneously in Madrid. he Middle East conference grabbed all the headlines and panish papers gave only scant coverage to the World ssembly on Ageing II.

In April 2002 I decided to visit several African countries. The official purpose of the visit was to observe the UN peacekeeping forces. There was no record of the President of the United Nations General Assembly ever having visited Africa in his official capacity. Ambassador Ban was eager to accompany me on this trip.

Like Africa, Korea had been underdeveloped. I wanted to visit the continent because I hoped to contribute to its development and felt profound sympathy for its people. I had included on my itinerary attendance and a speech at the New Partnership for Africa's Development (NEPAD) summit meeting. Prior to leaving for Africa, I had to receive six injections at the UN medical clinic and was given a bag containing a variety of drugs. Until then, I had not known that visiting Africa required so many injections and drugs.

My visit to Africa began in Ghana. Ghana had made 2,000 of its 7,000 soldiers available to the UN for peacekeeping operations in Sierra Leone and Lebanon. I arrived in Ghana on the night of 11 April 2002. The Ghanaian President, John A. Kufuor, sent his brother, Defense Minister Addo-Kufuor, and the Foreign Minister to greet me at the airport. Dr. Addo-Kufuor is a physician and was a medical student at Cambridge University at about the time I was teaching there. We headed for the President's official residence.

I had met President John Kofi Agyekum Kufuor at the Nobel Prize Award Ceremony in Oslo the previous December, so we were old acquaintances. I expressed my deep appreciation for Ghana's dispatch of troops to UN peacekeeping operations. President Kufuor invited me to make some comments to the reporters covering our meeting. I responded as follows:

> Ever since I was inaugurated as the President of the UN General Assembly, I have made African development my top priority. I wanted to visit Ghana before visiting anywhere else. Ghana is the homeland of Secretary-General Annan. He and I share a bond of friendship and trust as we work closely for the peace and prosperity of the world. I would like to express my appreciation to the Ghanaian people for their support of the UN peacekeeping forces and their active contribution and cooperation to global peace.

President Kufuor sincerely welcomed the visit of the President of the United Nations General Assembly. He noted that when Ghana gained independence in 1957, Korea and Ghana were at almost the same stage economically. Forty years later, Ghana's national per capita income still remains at about $300, whereas that of Korea has reached $10,000. He said that he would like to know the secret of Korea's successful economic development. He also expressed his respect to the President of the General Assembly for making the effort to visit Africa to see firsthand what the issues are. He concluded by saying that he could not understand why none of my predecessors at the United Nations had come to Africa to see the realities of the continent.

The following day we left Accra for Sierra Leone. The UN Mission in Sierra Leone (UNAMSIL) was headquartered at Mammy Yoko Hotel in Freetown, the capital. Special Representative of the Secretary-General of the United Nations Oluyemi Adeniji of Nigeria, Deputy Representatives Behrooz Sadry of Iran, Alan Doss of the United Kingdom, and Force

91

Commander and Chief Military Observer General Daniel Opande of Kenya greeted me.

After taking a rest at the UNAMSIL office, we went to the President's official residence. A man of great physical stature, President Ahmad Tejan Kabbah had in the past served as UNDP Director of Personnel. He was reinstated as President after the civil war and in 1999, in parallel with these developments, the UN Mission was set up. A ceasefire was agreed to in November 2000, at which time the UN force was fully deployed. In January 2002 the UN approved the establishment of the Special Court for Sierra Leone to try those responsible for atrocities committed during the civil war. President Kabbah expressed his gratitude for the UN's contribution to maintaining political stability and peace in his country.

We returned to the hotel where, beginning at 3:30 PM, I was briefed by the UNAMSIL staff. Conditions in Sierra Leone were stabilizing, and presidential and general elections were scheduled for May 2002. Recognizing the valuable role played by the UN forces, the Security Council had decided to extend its presence for six months, until 30 September. The Representative and Force Commander urged that it be extended even further. Because UN peacekeeping operations lie within the purview of the Security Council, as President of the General Assembly I had no authority to make any promises. I responded that when compared to UN peacekeeping operations elsewhere, the UN forces in Sierra Leone had produced substantial results and that I would be certain to convey their request to the Security Council and give it my support.

On 13 April General Opande took us to the midland region, where resistance of the rebel forces had been most intense. We flew in a helicopter provided by the Ukraine and piloted by a Ukrainian airman. I was given a briefing at the local battalion headquarters, where I noticed that the UN flag displayed was dirty and without a flagpole. It gave me the impression that the UN's standing and authority had been greatly compromised.

We visited the site of another hard-fought battle, Magburaka, where Bangladeshi troops were now stationed. There was a field hospital at Magburaka and hundreds of patients greeted us with waving hands. When I began shaking hands with them, they swarmed around me. I found myself shaking hands endlessly, like a candidate running for office. They were caring, pure-hearted people who had to endure suffering and misery because of the lack of political leadership. The area is well known for its diamonds. If effectively exploited, this rich resource could bring affluence, but it was this very resource that had caused the civil war that had claimed the lives of or maimed so many people.

A former leader of the rebel forces had been invited to the luncheon hosted by the Bangladeshi force. His rank had been brigadier general. He had joined the rebels at the age of 17 and fought for 11 years. Now he was engaged in agriculture as well as in children's education. He exuded an undefeatable will and struck me as being the most competent and resourceful person I met in Sierra Leone. I encouraged him, saying that education was a far more important endeavor than armed revolution.

New Partnership for Africa's Development (NEPAD) Meeting

After my visit to Sierra Leone, I went to Senegal via Gambia, which was a paradise compared with war-fatigued Sierra

Leone. As a professional economist brought up in a poor country, I was very much interested in the economic challenges facing developing countries, particularly in Africa. The fact that Secretary-General Annan was from Ghana also deepened my interest in the region. Immediately upon learning that I would be elected the President of the 56th Session of the United Nations General Assembly, I had instructed my office to give African development high priority and had instructed my staff to explore the role that could be played by the President to eradicate poverty and promote development in Africa.

Needless to say, the terrorist attacks of 11 September 2001 compelled us to significantly reorder our priorities. Responding to terrorism and reforming the UN had made the greatest demands on our time and attention, but I continued to hope to be able to contribute in some way to Africa's economic development. My travels to Sierra Leone to observe the operations of the UN peacekeeping force were a realization of this desire.

I was fortunate to be in Africa at that juncture, when the New Partnership for Africa's Development (NEPAD) meeting was being held in Dakar, Senegal. I looked forward to the opportunity this would provide to meet with African leaders and exchange views on economic development.

I arrived in Senegal on the second day of the NEPAD meeting. This meeting had been organized by the leaders of African countries, including President Abdoulaye Wade of Senegal, President Thabo Mbeki of South Africa, and President Olusegun Obasanjo of Nigeria, without the intervention of outside organizations. The leaders of 53 African nations were in attendance. President Wade and other proponents of the meeting were later invited to the G8 Summit in 2003 for expanded dialogue meetings.

Secretary-General Annan did not attend the NEPAD meeting, although President Wade told me he had personally called him twice to ask him to participate. The Secretary-General had declined and instead sent Mr. Kingsley Amoako, Executive Secretary of the UN Economic Commission for Africa with a congratulatory message from the Secretary-General. Disappointed by Annan's response, President Wade angrily turned down the message and banned the Executive Secretary from attending the meeting. It was under these circumstances that I attended the meeting as the President of the United Nations General Assembly and was therefore welcomed with great enthusiasm.

The heart of the agenda for the meeting was the encouragement of private investment. Securing funding from the private sector is essential for African development. The conference debated the best means of encouraging private businesses to invest in Africa. Approximately 500 business leaders attended.

The substance of my speech at the Senegal meeting was the same as the one I had given in Monterrey. I stressed that the essential elements for rapid growth in a developing country were stable funding from both domestic and foreign sources, fostering human capital and talent, the elimination of corruption, sound macroeconomic policies, and the rule of law. I also called for transparent politics and good public governance.

President Obasanjo followed me with a closing speech. He declared that there was no reason for the world's businesses not to invest in Africa, when the rate of return on investment was in the range of 30 to 35 percent. He also criticized the fact that business leaders of African origin often showed little enthusiasm for investing in Africa.

Indeed, why does Africa attract so little investment, despite a high rate of return? It seems likely that political instability and resulting uncertainty override the attraction of potential profit. Businesspeople seem to find even this high rate of return insufficient to make up for the threat of losses from political factors.

Representatives of the host governments commented that my speech clarified NEPAD's challenges and contributed to its credibility. The businesspeople attending the meeting also welcomed it, finding my message to African nations unambiguous and appropriate.

East Timor Independence Ceremony

On 18 March 2002 I received a letter from Secretary-General Annan asking me to accompany him to East Timor's independence celebration to be held in Dili in May. He wished to send a message to the world regarding the solidarity of the United Nations with the people of East Timor and the international community's welcome of the newly independent state. Of course, I agreed to attend.

The celebration was held on 19–20 May. We flew from Bali to the East Timorese capital of Dili. We made the flight in a UN-chartered aircraft, a very old deHavilland-7. On board were 32 passengers, including Annan and his wife.

I have attended many conferences and ceremonies as the President of the UN General Assembly, but none moved me more eeply than this celebration of East Timor's independence. It alled to mind the situation of Korea a half-century earlier when general election had been held in the South under UN supervi- ion, leading finally to recognition by the UN General Assembly s the only legitimate government on the Korean Peninsula. It was ntensely emotional to consider the situation in East Timor hrough the lens of my life experience in a war-torn country. At ne request of the United Nations, Korea had sent troops to be art of the international peacekeeping force in East Timor. When his dispatch of troops was being debated by Korea's National ssembly, there were some members who opposed sending roops to East Timor. As a Member of the National Assembly, I ad strongly supported the dispatch, and now I also wished to ee for myself how the Korean troops were performing.

The heat in Dili was nearly unbearable. No adequate ac- ommodations were available, and we had to stay on a pas- enger ship donated by the Swedish government and docked n the harbor. Many dignitaries attended the ceremony, includ- ng former US President Bill Clinton, as a special envoy from he United States. The Presidents of the World Bank and the Asian Development Bank also attended.

The venue of the official independence celebration cere- nony was overflowing with people and with an intense mood of oy. It was profoundly touching to see the fighters in the inde- endence struggle enter and march before us. Former guerrillas lragging a wounded leg or missing an arm, soldiers who ooked as young as children, women of considerable age—as hese heroes of independence greeted us from before the stage, could not contain my emotion.

This country, with a population of less than one million, ad fought for its independence from Indonesia for 25 years, losing 200,000 people in the process. I was moved to be a witness to the human dignity and the independence won at the cost of so many lives.

Nobel Peace laureate and Foreign Minister Ramos Horta introduced the dignitaries representing each country and then, at 12:00 AM, on 20 May, the moment of independence arrived. I spoke first to make a congratulatory address on behalf of the United Nations. In my speech, I gave voice to the profound emotions that had been stirred in me by what I had seen there. Because English is not one of East Timor's official languages, I had assumed that I would not be understood, but my speech was interrupted by at least five rounds of applause. I was overwhelmed. I felt from the audience the kind of emotion that could be experienced only by a people who had gone through the same pain and suffering as Koreans.

Former President Clinton later sought me out and shook my hand, telling me that mine was a fantastic speech. Although we are not close, we have known each other for some years. President Clinton had received me and my family when I went to present my credentials to him in the White House in June 1993. I was sent to Washington, D.C. as Korean Ambassador to the United States the previous April.

How can East Timor develop in the future? Annan and I discussed this matter at length during our flight and at the East Timor National Parliament hall. What kind of support should the UN give? Our discussion went on and on, and we lost all track of time. I described the cases of Korea and many developing countries and offered my own conclusion: a developing country whose leaders avoided injustice and corruption had a hopeful future. Annan could not have agreed more.

Chapter 6: Revitalizing the General Assembly

Regional Groups Choose the President

According to the United Nations Charter, the General Assembly is one of six principal organs of the UN, the others being the Security Council, the Economic and Social Council, the Trusteeship Council, the International Court of Justice, and the Secretariat. The General Assembly is, however, the largest organ representing the Member States, which includes virtually all the countries of the world. In this sense, it serves the function of a global parliament or congress.

Although the President is given the role of formally representing the United Nations, the Secretary-General exercises authority over such matters as personnel and budget and in this sense functions as the actual representative of the UN. The Secretary-General traditionally serves two five-year terms.

It is customary that neither the President nor the Secretary-General be chosen from among the Member States with permanent seats on the Security Council. Thus, the United States, the United Kingdom, France, Russia, and China are not supposed to nominate their nationals to these positions.

The President's physical presence at the UN is not necessarily required at all times throughout the year. Except for four months, from September to December, the workload of the General Assembly becomes less pressing and from January, even Foreign Ministers can hold both posts without much difficulty. Of the 56 Presidents to date, 18 have been Foreign Ministers, three Vice Foreign Ministers, 24 Permanent Representatives at the UN, two Ambassadors to the United States, and six current or past Prime Ministers or Presidents.

How is the President chosen? Currently—and this differs from the modality used in the early years of the UN—selection is made on a rotating basis from within the five regional groups: Asia, Africa, Eastern Europe, Latin America and the Caribbean, and Western Europe and others. Each group is free to choose from among its constituent countries the candidate the members feel is most appropriate. As of 2001, the Asian group consists of 50 countries and Africa has 53, while Eastern Europe has 21 and Latin America and the Caribbean 33. The Western Europe and others group consists of 27 countries, while the USA, Estonia, Kiribati, Palau, and Tuvalu do not belong to any regional groups. When the regional group responsible for choosing that year's President has selected the Member State to nominate the President, it is customary for the General Assembly to elect the President thus selected by acclamation. When consensus cannot be reached on nominating one candidate within the pertinent regional group, the General Assembly holds an election to select the President.

As of 2001, there had been 13 Presidents from Asia, including myself (Korea), the Philippines (4th Session), Iran (5th Session), India (8th Session), Thailand (11th Session), Pakistan (18th Session), Afghanistan (21st Session), Indonesia (26th Session), Sri Lanka (31st Session), Iraq (36th Session), Bangladesh (41st Session), Saudi Arabia (46th Session), and Malaysia (51st Session). Each year, 21 Vice Presidents are chosen to support the President's work; five of them are from each of the five permanent members of the Security Council. For the 56th Session of the General Assembly, there were, in addition to the permanent five, four Vice Presidents from Asia, six from Africa, three from the Latin America and Caribbean region, one from Eastern Europe, and two from Western Europe and others. Similar to the process of selection for the President, the Vice Presidents are selected by their respective regional groups and are elected in the General Assembly by acclamation.

The Vice Presidents have dual duties as the Ambassadors of their governments at the United Nations. When the President returns or is called back to his or her home country, or is away for official duties, the Vice Presidents nominated by the President preside over meetings held by the General Assembly and attend any ceremonial functions where they are required.

The General Committee and Internal Groups

On 14 September 2001, the third day of the General Assembly session, I convened a meeting of the General Committee in Conference Room 4 in the basement. The General Committee deals with all of the procedural issues that arise in connection with the operation of the General Assembly. In addition to the President and the 21 Vice Presidents, the General Committee includes representatives of the six major committees of the General Assembly, for a total of 28 members. This is an important body that determines which agenda items will be put before the General Assembly.

Just as national parliaments have within them various committees, the United Nations General Assembly has six main committees. By custom, the chairs of the respective committees are allocated to the respective regional groups. The

101

nominees of the regional groups are elected by acclamation on the second day of the session.

The first topic of discussion of the General Committee is how to determine agenda items. In the case of the 56th Session of the General Assembly, a total of 189 agenda items were carried over from the previous year's session, virtually all of which were subject to being adopted without debate. Each year, it is customary for many agenda items from the previous year's session to be recognized in this way as agenda items for the next year.

The question of whether or not to include Taiwan as a UN Member State is one concern that has caused much debate over the years. In 2001, a total of 89 Member States sought opportunity to address the issue. Needless to say, if all 89 requests were accepted, the time required for speeches would have been considerable and would have placed a great burden on the General Committee. Because I had heard from my predecessor that the meetings of the General Committee that dealt with this question had been known to continue into the early morning hours of the following day, I was prepared for the issue to be very time-consuming.

The representative of Guiana and other countries spoke at great length to urge that the question of Taiwan's UN membership be taken up by the General Assembly. In comparison, speeches opposing the matter were brief. As might be expected, the representative of China explained the reasons for his government's opposition to this idea, but he did so very succinctly.

While a considerable amount of time was dedicated to discussing the issue, it was, perhaps due to the impact of the terrorist attacks of only a few days earlier, more abbreviated than in previous years. It was possible to conclude the meeting of the General Committee in the evening, without having it drag on late into the night.

In addition to the chairs of the respective regional groups, the so-called internal groups exert considerable influence over the actual functioning of the General Assembly. There are five such groups, and it is virtually impossible to maintain the smooth operation of the General Assembly without attending to their views. These groups also work together to lobby for different visions of Security Council reform.

The internal groups are: the Group of 77, comprising developing countries, numerically the largest of the groups, and China; the five permanent members of the Security Council—the so-called "P5"—whose interests regularly clash within the Security Council but who will work together to protect their common interests when there are differences with the General Assembly, such as over reform of the Security Council; and the Rio Group, comprised of Latin American countries, the European Union, and nonaligned nations.

Revitalizing the General Assembly

When a candidate is selected to the post of the President of the United Nations General Assembly, the criteria for election are not dependent upon how much knowledge the candidate has on international affairs or how much experience he has accumulated in the area of foreign policy. If that were the objective, the government in question would have to appoint past or current UN ambassadors or someone with intimate knowledge of UN affairs. However, governments tend to nominate candidates on the basis of the prevailing dynamics of their domestic politics. They may appoint someone with strong domestic standing and who is capable of working within the domestic political situation. For these reasons, the nominee may not necessarily be familiar with international affairs in general and the United Nations in particular.

Thus, many of those elected to serve as the President learn "on the job" as they proceed to fulfill the actual responsibilities of the presidency. The busiest period for the General Assembly is during the first four months of any session, from September through December. The intensity of activity during this period means that newly elected Presidents of the General Assembly have no opportunity to study or learn about their job in a leisurely or paced manner. They must learn on the run, improvising responses as they go along.

Many Presidents are also Foreign Ministers at home and are frequently required to travel back and forth between their home country and New York, making it impossible for them to be at UN Headquarters uninterruptedly. This also makes it difficult for Presidents to focus exclusively on the business of the General Assembly.

The General Assembly has made efforts over the years to strengthen and make more effective its functioning as one of the principal organs of the United Nations. In many ways, the same pressures that work for the reform of the Security Council can be seen in the case of strengthening and revitalizing the General Assembly.

A number of conferences and meetings have been held to discuss the question of how best to revitalize the General Assembly. An informal meeting to seriously discuss this issue was held in Conference Room 1 on 16 May 2002. I asked Ambassador Juan Gabriel Valdez, Permanent Representative of Chile, to act as a facilitator for the meeting. This was because he had facilitated discussions on reforming and strengthening the General Assembly in the previous session. Ambassador Valdez, however, told me that this was an impossible task for him to fulfill single-handedly and asked me to increase the number of facilitators. Chile was already on the Economic and Social Council and was seeking to become a non-permanent member of the Security Council. These matters kept him very busy, but recognizing the importance of discussions to revitalize the work of the General Assembly, he agreed to take on the responsibility if I increased the number of facilitators. I responded to his request by appointing representatives of four other countries as facilitators: Ambassador Jean-David Levitte of France, Ambassador Kishore Mahbubani of Singapore, Ambassador Hynek Kmonicek of the Czech Republic, and Ambassador Dumisani Sahdrak Kumalo of South Africa. They were chosen on the basis of geographical representation, as well as their ability to bring together the views of the Member States.

Two proposals were circulated regarding enhancing the efficiency of the work of the President, who may not be well versed in the workings of the United Nations at the time of inauguration. The first proposal, made by Brazil, was to have the presidency's one-year term run from 1 January to the end of the calendar year. This would allow the President's term to begin at a time when the General Assembly was least busy and would give the President more time to gain an understanding of the nature of the post and to get used to the job. The second proposal was to start the term of the President several months prior to the start of the year's session, in order to give the President sufficient time to learn and prepare for the demands of the position.

Of these two proposals, the second attracted more support. The question then became, how many months of lead-time should be allowed the incoming President? There were many voices supporting the idea that three months would be adequate, but in the case of the 57th Session, it was agreed that the incoming President would be elected two months before the start of the year's session. This was because the revision of the rules of procedures would take time. It was also agreed that the 21 Vice Presidents and chairs of the major committees who comprise the General Committee would be chosen at the same time. This agreement was achieved after four meetings, in which the support of the respective regional groups was gained. As a result, it was decided to revise the rules of procedure of the General Assembly for the first time.

On 28 June word was received from Russia, which was that month's chair of the East European group, that they wished to nominate Jan Kaban, Deputy Prime Minister and Minister of Foreign Affairs of the Czech Republic, as a sole candidate to be the President of the 57th Session of the General Assembly. Until that time, Belarus was contending the candidacy and did not withdraw its intention to compete. On 8 July the General Assembly was convened to adopt the revised rules and elect the President of the 57th Session of the General Assembly. Deputy Prime Minister Kaban of the Czech Republic was unanimously elected to be the next President of the General Assembly, and Articles 30, 31, and 99 of the General Assembly's rules of procedure were duly revised.

On 8 July I met with the incoming President and discussed a wide range of issues with him. The staff of his Presidential Office had already arrived in New York and met twice with my staff to be briefed on a variety of work-related issues. I myself had taken up my post as the President of the United Nations General Assembly with virtually no preparation, so I was proud of this systemic reform, which I feel was one of my contributions to the revitalization of the United Nations General Assembly.

Davos in New York

The World Economic Forum in Davos, named for the resort town in Switzerland where it is held each winter, is a privately organized conference of the highest authority that brings together world-class political leaders, high-ranking government officials, international businesspeople, and scholars. For 2002, it was decided to hold the Davos meeting in New York, beginning on 31 January. The choice of venue was an expression of solidarity, to encourage and to boost the morale of the citizens of New York, who had been victimized by the terrorist attacks.

On 1 February, a symposium on "Constructing Solidarity for a Stable World" was held at the Waldorf-Astoria Hotel. I was invited to be one of seven panelists. The others were US Secretary of State Colin Powell, the Secretary-General of the North Atlantic Treaty Organization (NATO), the EU High Representative for the common foreign and security policy, and the Foreign Ministers of Australia, France, and Turkey.

In my presentation, I explained the role that the United Nations played following the September 11 attacks. The United Nations responded quickly by adopting strong resolutions in both the General Assembly and the Security Council, condemning terrorism and expressing its solidarity with the people of the United States. Then the UN General Assembly demonstrated an unprecedented interest in the issue by holding a debate on the measures to eliminate international terrorism, in which the representatives of 167 countries spoke. Mayor Giuliani was invited to become the first Mayor of New York City to address the General Assembly. The Security Council also passed a resolution authorizing intervention in Afghanistan to punish the Taliban regime, which was aiding and refusing to turn over al-Qaeda terrorists. After explaining the UN's aggressive response to terrorism, I made the following appeal:

> The United Nations has thus made great contributions to solidarity for a stable world at the time of international crisis. Finally, I would like to share the words of the chair of the Nobel Peace Committee at the time of awarding the Nobel Peace Prize to the United Nations in Oslo on 10 December last year. He said, 'It is the way of the United Nations to bring peace and security to the world through negotiations.' Investments to strengthen the United Nations are quality investments in a more peaceful and secure world. I would hope that you, who are here today, particularly the international business leaders, would devote even so little as a minute each day to thinking about how you can help and cooperate with the United Nations.

After the symposium was over, and as I stepped down from the podium, I saw Bishop Gunnar Stalsett of Oslo, the Vice Chairman of the Norwegian Nobel Committee, enthusiastically waving in my direction. I was taken aback as I did not expect to see him there in New York. He approached me and expressed his gratitude as, he said, I helped enhance the reputation of the Nobel Peace Committee by my reference to the remarks made by its chair in Oslo.

Epilogue

The World Economic Forum puts out a bimonthly publication titled Economic Link. Every year it announces a so-called Dream Cabinet. In their November–December 2001 issue, they carried a special on the Dream Cabinet. Together with Secretary of State Powell, they chose me as Foreign Minister on the Dream Cabinet for the year.

Ambassador Ban Ki-moon, the Chef de Cabinet to the President of the 56th Session of the United Nations General Assembly, who later became Korea's Foreign Minister, was recommended unanimously by the Security Council to the post of the 8th Secretary-General of the United Nations, and the General Assembly approved the nomination by acclamation on 13 October 2006.

Appendix I: Major Speeches as the President of the UN General Assembly

i. Acceptance Speech on 12 September 2001

President Holkeri, Secretary-General Annan, Excellencies, Distinguished Delegates, Ladies and Gentlemen:

It is with a most grave and solemn mind that I take this podium, as the horrific events of yesterday cast a pall over our proceedings today. Mere words cannot express the outrage and disgust we doubtless all feel for the vile actions perpetrated in our host country, the United States of America. I condemn in the strongest possible terms these heinous acts of terrorism. I pray for those who lost their lives and on behalf of the UN General Assembly offer our deepest condolences to the families and loved ones of the innocent victims. My most profound feelings of sympathy and solidarity also go out to the people and government of the United States as well as to the citizens of New York City at this time of great distress.

These terrorist crimes were, in effect, acts of war against all the world's peace-loving peoples. Their primary target was, by a vicious twist of fate, located in the very city which is home to the world's foremost institution dedicated to promoting world peace. The opening of this session of the General Assembly has been delayed by a day due to this tragedy. But no terrorists can ever deflect this body from the task to which it has dedicated itself since 1945—ending the scourge of war in whatever form it may take once and for all.

Now let me share with you my vision of the work of the 56th Session of the General Assembly. At the outset, I would like to express sincere gratitude to my distinguished predecessor, His Excellency Mr. Harri Holkeri, whose outstanding leadership was instrumental in making the 55th Session highly successful. I wish President Holkeri all the best in his future endeavors. I would also like to pay tribute to the Secretary-General, His Excellency Mr. Kofi Annan, for his untiring efforts and selfless dedication to the highest ideals of the United Nations. I would like to take this opportunity to thank all the Member States, particularly the Asian Group countries, for the confidence they have placed in me.

As I begin my term of office, I have profoundly mixed feelings. While I am overwhelmed by the honor accorded me and my country, I feel at the same time a tremendous burden of responsibility. This is particularly so as I come from a country that has had a long and unique relationship with the United Nations. Indeed, the UN has been closely involved with my country since the establishment of the Republic of Korea in 1948 through the post–Korean War recovery period and the economic development of later years.

Following the end of the Cold War, the Republic of Korea joined the UN in 1991. I would like to believe that my election to this post, coinciding with the 10th anniversary of Korea's admission to the UN, constitutes a recognition by the Member States of Korea's increased contribution to the international community.

Fifty-six years ago, the United Nations was born amid hopes for a lasting peace in the wake of two devastating world wars. In the Charter, the UN's founding fathers set forth lofty goals and principles aimed at promoting international peace and security as well as the economic and social advancement of all peoples. Success was never easy, and failure often seemed inevitable. However, with its record of both successes and failures, the United Nations has come to be regarded as the sole universal body representing humanity's highest collective aspirations.

When the Cold War ended a decade ago, the international community faced new challenges and opportunities. As the danger of global conflict receded, the world was confronted with new threats to peace and development, such as regional and sectarian conflicts and the kinds of terrorist acts that reached a crescendo of violence yesterday.

At the same time, the tide of globalization surges ever onward, bringing both benefits and problems in its wake. While greater interdependence and increased cross-border movement have dramatically enhanced the well-being of mankind in many ways, there is a negative side as well: a growing problem of disease and pollution, recurring financial crises, and increasing cross-border crime, especially trafficking of drugs, weapons, and illegal migrants. In several of these areas, various UN agencies have been active for decades. Now, more than ever before, the UN is required to serve as a focal point for coordinating global efforts to address these new challenges.

In this context, I would like to emphasize the importance of the Millennium Summit held in this august chamber last year. The Summit provided a unique opportunity to review the UN's progress, to assess its achievements and shortcomings, and to chart the way forward. The Millennium Declaration adopted at the end of the Summit is surely the definitive statement of the challenges and tasks facing the UN at this stage in its history. As this is the first session of the General Assembly following the Millennium Summit, one of our most important tasks will be follow-up and implementation of the Millennium Declaration.

We all recognize that an important element of the Millennium Declaration is the resolve of the leaders to strengthen the United Nations. I think it is noteworthy that they reaffirmed the central position of the General Assembly as the chief deliberative, policy-making, and representative organ of the UN. As President of the 56th Session of the General Assembly, I will continue the ongoing initiatives to improve the working methods of the Assembly in close consultation with all Member States. I will also do my best to move forward the discussions on Security Council reform with the goal of having a more representative, transparent, and effective Security Council.

Given the fundamental changes in the international environment, the UN's role in maintaining peace and security has expanded and become more complex. I, therefore, attach great importance to improving the UN's capacity to respond to conflicts in a more effective manner, including consideration of the recommendations contained in the Brahimi Report. If it is to do its job of maintaining international peace and security, the United Nations needs to be given the necessary tools and resources for carrying out peace operations.

Also at the Millennium Summit, the world's leaders pledged their best efforts to promote democracy and strengthen the rule of law and to expand protection of human ights and fundamental freedoms. Freedom and human rights are truly the birthright of all humanity. This Assembly has to work continuously to promote the human rights of all people. But some categories of human beings are more vulnerable than others and hence more likely to suffer the loss of this precious birthright. Perhaps the most vulnerable are children, women, and displaced persons, who need our special concern and protection.

The United Nations should also strengthen and expand its efforts to prevent and suppress terrorism. All forms of terrorism—whatever their motivation—are an assault on human decency and threaten democratic values and, thus, cannot be justified under any circumstances. Yesterday's terrorist attacks not only compel our attention but underscore anew the urgency of action by the international community, particularly by the United Nations, against this deadly menace. I pledge my best efforts to this end.

In view of the accelerating process of globalization and the uneven sharing of its benefits, the issue of development is receiving renewed attention and is being considered from fresh perspectives. More specifically, the question of how to ensure that the developing countries share in the benefits of globalization in general, and of information and communication technology in particular, requires our urgent consideration and action. In this regard, I would like to call your attention to a couple of the most important issues to command our attention during my presidency of the General Assembly. They are bridging the digital divide and the development of Africa.

The explosive growth of information and communication technologies (ICT) is opening up boundless new possibilities for accelerated economic and social development. But the capacity of individual countries to take advantage of the digital revolution varies greatly. Indeed, the least developed countries that could gain so much from ICT are the very ones that lack the capacity to translate this potential into reality.

In my view, the General Assembly can make useful contributions by calling global attention to the need for bridging the digital divide. Such efforts by the General Assembly would be especially timely and constructive in the run-up to the World Summits on Information Society in 2003 and 2005 planned by the International Telecommunication Union.

In their Millennium Declaration, the world's leaders expressed their deep concern and highlighted the need to bring Africa into the mainstream of world economic development in the common interest of all humanity. The governments and peoples of Africa, together with the United Nations system and the donor community, have striven for decades to eradicate poverty and generate sustainable development. Yet all too often their best efforts have met with setbacks caused by political strife, armed conflict, and, since the 1980s, the devastating spread of HIV/AIDS.

Fortunately, the recent OAU Summit Meeting held in Lusaka, Zambia, gave a clear political lead on this issue through the New African Initiative. I urge that all Member States continue to work together to explore more effective ways and means of assisting African countries in their pursuit of sustainable development. Having outlined my agenda, I am confident that, working together, we can accomplish what we set out to do. My personal contribution will necessarily be a modest one. All these endeavors, to which I will devote myself, will be difficult to bring to fruition without the full support and cooperation of all of you. Thus, I humbly ask you to give me your invaluable support and guidance in discharging my duty as President of the General Assembly.

Finally, allow me to suggest that at this point in history, we should harken back to the original spirit and principles of the United Nations. Let us place first, before anything else, the transcendent vision enshrined in the Charter: namely, the constant and untiring pursuit of peace, security, equality, human rights, fundamental freedoms, and economic and social advancement for all the people on this planet. While respecting the sovereign rights and legitimate national interests of all nations, let us strive to make our common future a worthy legacy for succeeding generations. Let us, moreover, seek harmony through diversity, peace through dialogue, and mutual prosperity through cooperation. And so, as we assemble here in the world's greatest parliament, let us rededicate ourselves to the founding principles of the United Nations and renew our commitment to complete the unfinished tasks that lie before us.

ii. "Measures to Eliminate International Terrorism"

5 October 2001

Excellencies, Distinguished Delegates:

We have had an unusually long but very important and constructive debate during the last five days. It is unprecedented in the history of the UN for 167 Member States and 4 Observers to participate in the debate on a single agenda item. This fact alone eloquently demonstrates how seriously all

Member States and the whole international community regard the acts of terrorism that took place on 11 September. It was because we all believed that they were not only attacks on the United States but assaults on the whole civilized world.

As we all know, this agenda item "Measures to Eliminate International Terrorism" (item 166) has long been on the agenda of the Sixth Committee. However, in light of the importance and urgency of the issue in the aftermath of the tragedy of 11 September, we decided that the debate on this item be held in plenary meetings while consideration of the technical aspects of the item remain within the purview of the Sixth Committee.

Before the beginning of our debate, we had an invaluable opportunity to listen to Mayor Rudolph Giuliani of New York, our host city, who gave us a very clear perspective on the terrorist attacks and conveyed the expectations that U.S. citizens, particularly the citizens of New York, have of the United Nations at this critical time. I would like to take this opportunity to thank him again and offer our very best wishes for our host city's speedy recovery.

During our deliberations, all participants joined wholeheartedly in condemning the terrorist attacks of 11 September, reaffirming General Assembly resolution 56/1 of 12 September 2001 in which the General Assembly condemned these attacks in the strongest terms and called for international cooperation to bring to justice the perpetrators, organizers, and sponsors of the outrages.

Member States voiced the view that international terrorism constitutes a threat to international peace and security as well as a crime against humanity. Undoubtedly, international terrorism is one of the most formidable challenges to the world community in the 21st century, and the United Nations should play the key role in intensifying international efforts to eliminate such terrorism.

In this regard, I wish to recall that the General Assembly has taken important steps by adopting the Declaration on Measures to Eliminate International Terrorism in 1994 and its supplementary Declaration in 1996. The Security Council has also taken initiatives such as the adoption of resolutions 1269 of 19 October 1999, 1368 of 12 September 2001, and 1373 of 28 September 2001, which not only condemned all forms of terrorism but also specified measures to be taken by Member States to prevent and suppress terrorist acts.

Member States recognized the urgency of dealing with all forms and manifestations of international terrorism and those who harbor and support the perpetrators, organizers, and sponsors of international terrorism. They stressed the need to enhance international cooperation and to promptly take all necessary measures to prevent and suppress terrorist activities.

Member States concurred in the view that a primary task facing the international community at present is to ensure that an effective legal framework for the prevention and elimination of international terrorism is in place. To this end, I call upon all Member States that have not yet done so to become, as a matter of priority, parties to the existing international conventions relating to terrorism. In this context, it is noteworthy that the Commission on Crime Prevention and Criminal Justice has recently adopted the revised Draft Action Plan for the Implementation of the Vienna Declaration on Crime and

Justice. Many Member States also expressed their intention to take necessary measures to implement international conventions within their domestic jurisdiction.

I would like to take this opportunity to urge Member States to accelerate the work of the General Assembly with a view to early conclusion of the pending conventions on international terrorism in order to enhance the capacity of the international community to combat terrorism. As President of the General Assembly, I also wish to kindly request the Sixth Committee to expedite its work and submit its report to the General Assembly as early as possible, preferably by 15 November 2001.

Finally, I recall that during our debate Member States shared the view that the international community should resolve to fight terrorism as a phenomenon separate from any religion or ethnic group. In this regard, the necessity of dialogue among civilizations was stressed. Also some delegates suggested a high-level conference on international terrorism, while some others called upon the international community to address the root causes of terrorism. At the same time, the need for a clearer definition of terrorism was raised for our further consideration.

Our week-long deliberation was instrumental in reaffirming the central role of the United Nations in dealing with global and high-profile issues such as international terrorism. It is my sincere hope that the United Nations and the international community will take further necessary measures to combat international terrorism, building on the deliberations we have had for the last five days.

Thank you.

iii. The Nobel Peace Prize 2001 Presentation Speech

Presentation Speech by Gunnar Berge, Chairman of the Norwegian Nobel Committee, Oslo, 10 December 2001. [Translation of the Norwegian text]

Your Majesty, Your Royal Highnesses, Excellencies, Ladies and Gentlemen, and, not least, this year's and past year's Peace Prize Laureates. Let me begin by extending a warm welcome to this year's special Peace Prize award ceremony.

The Nobel Peace Prize for 2001 is awarded to the United Nations (the UN) and its Secretary-General Kofi Annan for their work for a better organized and more peaceful world.

This year we are celebrating the centenary of the Nobel Prizes, including the Peace Prize. That makes it natural to consider historical continuities where both the better organized world and the Nobel Peace Prize are concerned. The idea that mankind has common interests, and that this should find expression in some form or other of shared government or rules, can be traced back to the Roman Empire. In the 20th century, Woodrow Wilson was a vigorous early spokesman for the belief that we people need each other. Such a belief means that, whether as states or as individuals, we should treat one another in ways that do not make us less able to live together. Tolerance, justice, and humanity are essential to the unity of mankind.

Alfred Nobel had no self-evident place in this tradition. At one time, he believed that dynamite, his great invention, could do more to prevent war than any peace movement.

Nevertheless, the will he made in 1895 was inspired by belief in the community of man. The Peace Prize was to be awarded to the person who had done most for "fraternity between nations, for the abolition or reduction of standing armies and for the holding and promotion of peace congresses."

Over the one hundred years that have passed since the first Peace Prize was awarded in 1901, the foremost sustained intention of the Norwegian Nobel Committee has been precisely that: of strengthening international cooperation between states. In the period before World War I, the majority of the Peace Prizes went to representatives of the organized peace movement, either at the parliamentary level through the Inter-Parliamentary Union or at the more popular level through the International Peace Bureau. But the prizes do not seem to have helped much. The First World War broke out in 1914.

In the words of Woodrow Wilson, the First World War was to be "the war to end wars" and should "make the world safe for democracy." The new League of Nations was to be the body that resolved conflicts before they led to war. Once again, the Norwegian Nobel Committee sought to promote this greater commitment in international cooperation. In the years between the wars, at least eight Peace Prize Laureates had clear connections with the League of Nations, although the League as such never in fact received the prize.

Again the world, and not least Wilson himself, was to be disappointed. The 1919 Peace Prize Laureate was unable to persuade his own United States to join the League of Nations. For would not binding obligations to an international organization also limit American sovereignty?

Practically all of us wish to avoid the horrors of war. But we have different notions about how this can come about. All non-pacifists seek other things in addition to peace. There is not necessarily anything wrong with that. Nor can peace be absolute. That was why so many took up arms against Hitler Germany and the Emperor's Japan.

The horrors of World War II made the hopes people pinned on the new world organization, the United Nations, all the greater. The new organization was set even higher targets than the League of Nations. The preamble to the UN Charter thus speaks of "We the peoples of the United Nations determined to save succeeding generations from the scourge of war, which twice in our lifetime has brought untold sorrow to mankind. . . ." There were many points of organizational similarity between the League of Nations and the UN. But the League of Nations had failed. The answer was to give the Security Council a much more prominent role than the corresponding council had had in the League of Nations. Universal membership would be combined with special rights exercised by the Great Powers. The Security Council could use military force to maintain peace. It was even to have standing armed forces at its disposal, to be established by Member States in cooperation. We have not reached that goal even today, 56 years on.

The UN has achieved many successes, not least in the humanitarian and social fields, where its various special organizations have done such important work. In some respects, the UN achieved more than its founders believed possible. It found itself in the thick of the process of decolonization, which in a few short decades swept away centuries-old colo-

nial empires. The UN set important standards, which influ
enced developments for the majority of people all over the
world. The Universal Declaration of Human Rights, adopted
by the UN in 1948, became one of the major documents o
our time. Article 1 gives clear expression to the hope for a bet
ter organized and more peaceful world: "All human beings are
born free and equal in dignity and human rights. They are en
dowed with reason and conscience and should act towards
one another in a spirit of brotherhood."

The Norwegian Nobel Committee has sought to give
these successes the credit they deserve. Since 1945, at least 13
of the Peace Prizes have had links to the UN. Some have gone
to UN organizations such as the High Commissioner for
Refugees, winner of two awards, UNICEF, the ILO, and the
UN's peacekeeping forces. Others have gone to individuals
like Cordell Hull, reputed to have provided the inspiration un
derlying the UN, John Boyd Orr, the first head of the FAO
Ralph Bunche, first of many UN mediators in the Middle East
and, in 1950, the first non-white Peace Prize Laureate, Dag
Hammarskjöld, the UN's second Secretary-General, and René
Cassin, main author of the Declaration of Human Rights.

In its most important area, however, preventing war and
ensuring peace, the UN did not turn out to be all that its sup
porters had hoped for. In many serious conflicts, the organiza
tion remained on the sidelines or was used as a tool by one o
the parties. The five Great Powers had all agreed that they had
to have a veto. But it is not the veto itself, of course, that ex
plains the UN's inability to act, but rather the fact that the in
terests of the two superpowers diverged so radically through
out the many years of the Cold War.

Seeing that the main theme in the history of the Peace Prize has been the wish for a better organized and more peaceful world, it is surprising that the UN as such has not been awarded the Peace Prize before. One reason may be disappointment that the UN did not quite live up to all the expectations of 1945. Another may be the many UN-related prizes, which made it less necessary to give the award to the organization itself. A good deal can be attributed to chance: the UN could have won the award so often that in the end it never did. Until a suitably important occasion arrived. In connection with this year's centenary, the Committee once again felt a need to emphasise the continuous theme of the history of the Peace Prize, the hope for a better organized and more peaceful world. Nothing symbolizes that hope, or represents that reality, better than the United Nations.

The end of the Cold War meant that the UN became able to play more of the role in security policy for which it was originally intended. The Great Powers still had diverging interests; so, too, of course, had the smaller states, but they had less impact on the international climate. Although the USA provides the clearest illustration, all countries are more or less selective in their attitudes to the UN. They favor an active UN when they need and see opportunities to obtain its support; but when the UN takes a different stance, they seek to limit its influence. Since the Cold War, however, greater and smaller powers have to a significant extent been able to unite in meeting the most serious common challenges: to prevent wars and conflicts; to stimulate economic development, especially in poor countries; to strengthen fundamental human rights; to promote a better environment; to fight epidemics; and, in the most recent common endeavor, to prevent international terrorism.

No one has done more than Kofi Annan to revitalize the UN. After taking office as the UN's seventh Secretary-General in January 1997, he managed in a very short time to give the UN an external prestige and an internal morale the likes of which the organization had hardly seen in its over 50-year history, with the possible exception of its very first optimistic years. His position within the organization has no doubt benefited from his having devoted almost all his working life to the UN. Experience in a bureaucracy is not always the best springboard for action and fresh approaches to the outside world, but Annan has brought about both. The UN structure has been tightened up and made more efficient. The Secretary-General has figured prominently in the efforts to resolve a whole series of international disputes: the repercussions of the Gulf War, the wars in the former Yugoslavia and especially in Kosovo, the status of East Timor, the war in the Congo, and the implementation of the UN resolutions concerning the Middle East and "land for peace."

On the basis of renewed emphasis on the Declaration of Human Rights, Annan has given the Secretary-General a more active part to play as a protector of those rights. Time and again, he has maintained that sovereignty is not a shield behind which member countries can hide their violations. He has shown the same activist approach to the struggle against HIV/AIDS, a struggle which he has called his "personal priority." Since the terrorist attack on New York and Washington on 11 September, he has urged that the UN must be given a leading part to play in the fight against international terrorism.

The Secretary-General's report on the role of the UN in the 21st century formed the basis for the UN's Millennium Declaration. Here, too, the agenda is ambitious: to put an end to poverty, to provide better education for the world's billions of people, to reduce HIV/AIDS, to protect the environment, and to prevent war and armed conflict.

The only one of the UN's previous six Secretaries-General who can be compared to Annan in personal force and historical importance is Dag Hammarskjöld, the organization's second Secretary-General and the recipient of the Nobel Peace Prize in 1961. For Kofi Annan, Dag Hammarskjöld has been a model. In his Hammarskjöld Memorial Lecture in September this year, Annan said, "There can be no better rule of thumb for a Secretary-General, as he approaches each new challenge or crisis, than to ask himself, 'how would Hammarskjöld have handled this?'" Annan is nevertheless more of a team player than Hammarskjöld was. In other respects, too, Annan goes further than Hammarskjöld could: "I suspect he would envy me the discretion I enjoy in deciding what to say, and what topics to comment on." This can occasionally be a bit much, however, even for Annan: "I find myself called on to make official statements on almost everything that happens in the world today, from royal marriages to the possibility of human cloning!"

Wars between states have grown quite rare in recent decades. This can be regarded as a victory for norms which the UN has stood for throughout its existence. But many wars are still fought in our time. The new development is that wars within states, civil wars, have become relatively more frequent. This is confronting the UN with major challenges. The UN has traditionally been a defender of the sovereignty of individual states. The principle of state sovereignty is laid down in the UN Charter, especially in Article 2.7., but even that Article contains a qualification: ". . . this principle shall not prejudice the application of enforcement measures under chapter VII" (the chapter on action to preserve peace). Now that we are attaching ever-increasing importance to "human security" and not just to the security of states, it makes little difference whether a life is lost in an international or a civil war.

If the UN is to prevent civil war, the question soon arises of intervention from outside. Many see intervention as equivalent to invasion. Small states are naturally afraid that big states will use it as a pretext for interfering in their domestic affairs. The policies of colonial powers in Africa and Asia, the Soviet Union's entries into Eastern Europe, and the USA's various interventions in the Western hemisphere all illustrate the need to protect the sovereignty of small states. On the other hand, the present situation, with civil wars in numerous countries, is a high price to pay for regarding state sovereignty as absolute. The massacres in Rwanda taught us all, and not least Annan, that the world does not necessarily get any better if one refrains from intervening. As Annan himself has said, we applaud the policeman who "intervenes" to stop a fight, or the teacher who tries to prevent bullying and fighting; and a doctor "intervenes" to save patients' lives: "A doctor who never intervenes has few admirers and probably even fewer patients." Where humanitarian concerns are uppermost, Doctors without Borders (MSF) in particular, the 1999 Laureate, has argued that the global community has "a duty to intervene", a principle which the UN General Assembly has accepted in several important resolutions.

The debate on "humanitarian intervention" raises difficult questions to which there are no pat answers, especially when the debate shifts from purely humanitarian to more political ground. Under Annan's leadership, the UN has shown itself willing to participate in this difficult discussion, with significant results in the last few years. Developments have taken a favorable turn in Kosovo, though there is still a long way to go. The UN played a leading part in the process which in a short space of time advanced East Timor from the status of a colony to, before long, that of an independent state. Maybe the 1996 Peace Prize awarded to Belo and Ramos-Horta also contributed. Today large and small states alike are almost competing in urging the UN to take the lead in developing Afghanistan away from a Taliban regime that has been a leading supporter of international terrorism and toward a broadly-based government that can lead the country back into the international community.

So we have already moved well into the discussion of what steps to take to achieve a better organized and more peaceful world in the next hundred years. It has been repeated again and again that the UN cannot become anything more than the world's ever so multifarious governments wish to make it. But in the light of the many common tasks that lie ahead, we must at least see to it that the very slowest movers among the nations are not allowed to set too much of the future pace. As globalization expands, the question will be asked even more loudly than at present of who is to manage this development and by what means. In the view of the Nobel Committee, that will be a task for the UN, if not in the form of a centralized world government then at least as the more efficient global instrument which the world so sorely needs.

For that to come about, it will help if nations as far as possible have a shared platform. Democracy is stronger today than at any time in history; over half of the world's population lives under democratic government. This marks a great victory for the principles in the Human Rights Declaration. One need go no further than back to the inter-war years, when democracy was a threatened species of government, to realize how dramatic this progress has been. Democracies rarely if ever go to war with each other.

The strong position of democracy today gives grounds for optimism. But much remains to be done, not least in the economic field. We have made very few advances in solidarity between countries that are growing ever richer and the many countries and individuals who either are not benefiting to the same extent from globalization or are even suffering from its economic and social consequences. The number of poor people in the world is ever-increasing.

There were many reverses in the 20th century, for the world as a whole and for the idea of a better organized and more peaceful world. Two world wars, and a cold war that lasted more than 40 years and spread into every corner of the world, set a limit to how optimistic we can feel about the future. On the other hand, we have witnessed a remarkable development, from the scattered and rather private peace initiatives at the previous turn of the century to the ever-stronger and more efficient United Nations we have today. The Norwegian Nobel Committee wishes both to honor the work that the UN and its Secretary-General Kofi Annan have already done and to encourage them to go ahead along the road to a still more forceful and dynamic United Nations.

14 December 2001

Excellencies, Ladies and Gentlemen:

As you know, I have just returned from Oslo, Norway, where I had the great honor to accept the 2001 Nobel Peace Prize on behalf of the United Nations. I was also honored to attend this occasion, along with Secretary-General Kofi Annan, who accepted the prize on his own behalf. Let me take this opportunity to congratulate all the "family members" of the entire UN system and pay tribute to our Secretary-General, Mr. Kofi Annan.

Since this was the first time that the United Nations as a whole was awarded the Nobel Peace Prize, I was especially pleased that the major UN organs and various agencies were well represented at the ceremony.

I wish that all of you—the representatives of the Member States—could have been there as well. The Nobel Peace Prize belongs to each of you as much as to any other member of the UN family.

Surely this award is meant to offer encouragement to the men and women of the United Nations in carrying out their work. Such encouragement will be especially welcome to the thousands of UN personnel who serve under extremely difficult conditions, often at grave risk to themselves. While we can be justly proud of what the United Nations has accomplished, we should also look ahead to the many daunting challenges that still lie before us, such as terrorism, poverty, drug abuse and trafficking, HIV/AIDS, and environmental degradation.

133

These challenges cannot be met by any single Member State or any single organization alone.

Since 1945, the international community and the peoples of the world have exerted their best efforts, often with high hopes, for the realization of global peace and well-being through the United Nations. Our efforts have not always been successful, nor our successes always permanent.

But we should not be discouraged. I have no doubt that, were it not for the United Nations, humankind could hardly have advanced so far as it has in realizing the vision of the UN's founding fathers in 1945. The indispensable role of the UN was clearly recognized by Chairman Berge of the Norwegian Nobel Committee, at the award ceremony in the following words: "The only negotiable route to global peace and cooperation goes by way of the United Nations."

Finally, let me mention that I will closely consult with the representatives of the Major Organs and Member States about how to utilize the prize money which the UN has received from the Nobel Committee.

In concluding my brief report, I join with you in celebrating the award of the 2001 Nobel Peace Prize as both recognition of past achievements and a spur to even greater efforts in the future.

v. Statement on the Occasion of the African Summit Conference on Partnership with the Private Sector for Financing Africa's Growth Through the New Partnership for Africa's Development

16 April 2002, Dakar, Senegal

President Wade, Distinguished Heads of State and Government, Excellencies, Ladies and Gentlemen:

I am honored to be present at the African Summit Conference on Partnership with the Private Sector for Financing Africa's Growth through the New Partnership for Africa's Development (NEPAD). First of all, I would like to express my deep appreciation to President Wade of the Republic of Senegal for hosting this Conference.

President Wade's leadership and dedication in promoting the development of Africa and, in particular, his contribution to launching NEPAD as one of its founders are a source of encouragement not only for Africans but also for the entire international community.

Mr. President,

Upon assuming the presidency of the 56th Session of the United Nations General Assembly last September, I set as one of my priorities the African development. To reinforce the importance of that agenda, I have chosen four West African states as the first countries that I visit officially as President of the United Nations General Assembly. After Ghana, Sierra Leone along with UNAMSIL and its field offices, and The Gambia, Senegal is the fourth and the last leg of my trip to

135

this region. I would report back to the General Assembly what I have observed during my trip through West Africa.

Mr. President,

Now, more than ever, the development of Africa constitutes one of the gravest challenges confronting the world. Nearly half of the people in sub-Saharan Africa live on less than one dollar per day. Africa's average income per capita is lower than at the end of the 1960s, while the continent accounts for only 1.7 percent of international trade. Increasingly, the consequences of this deteriorating situation are being felt not just by Africans but also by the peoples and governments throughout the world.

Globalization has brought enormous opportunities and benefits through the expansion of markets, investment, and information flows across national borders. However, increased marginalization of the least developed countries in the globalizing world, most of them in Africa, endangers the future of the global community.

Mr. President,

At the UN Millennium Assembly, leaders of the world endorsed a set of international development targets. These include reducing by half the proportion of the world's population living in poverty, provision of universal primary education, and a two-thirds reduction in child mortality—all to be achieved by 2015. I believe that the Monterrey Consensus adopted at the International Conference on Financing for Development in Mexico last month added to a solid basis for pursuing these internationally agreed development targets.

At the Monterrey Conference, world leaders shared the view that both the rich and the poor countries should make common endeavors to eradicate poverty. Overwhelming support was expressed from the floor for NEPAD, which so clearly manifests the determination of African leaders to bring new hope and inspiration to the development of their continent through political and economic governance. As its name indicates, NEPAD aims to achieve its ambitious goals by forging partnerships—both among Africans themselves and between African states, the G-8, and the rest of the world.

I am very pleased to report to you that many participating countries at the Monterrey Conference encouraged and supported the early implementation of NEPAD. I believe that the acronym NEPAD is now becoming a watchword of regional development.

Mr. President,

Drawing on my own experience as Korea's Minister of Trade and Industry, Minister of Finance and Economy, and, most recently, Minister of Foreign Affairs and Trade, and more importantly, from the experience of Korea's economic development, I laid out three preconditions, in my opening remarks in Monterrey, for any country to achieve rapid and sustainable economic development. They are: first, access to financial resources, domestic or external; second, the necessary human capacity to efficiently absorb those resources; and, third, appropriate intangible infrastructure, such as a free market, good governance, sound macroeconomic policies, a strong anticorruption ethic, and transparently applied rule of law. In particular, these elements of intangible infrastructure are crucial in attracting foreign direct investment and other private capital flows into developing countries.

One of the major reasons for my optimism regarding NEPAD is that it incorporates all of these preconditions in its strategy for development. African states can begin to implement the ideals of NEPAD by formulating proper national development strategies and by establishing an appropriate mechanism to monitor and review the progress in human rights, and political and economic governance, among others.

Mr. President,

To promote the economic development of Africa, the political leadership and commitment of the African leaders is of critical importance. From this perspective, today's NEPAD summit meeting can provide a powerful momentum for both developed and developing countries to seriously engage in substantive discussions on the development of Africa. This coming September, the United Nations General Assembly will hold a high-level plenary meeting to discuss ways to support the New Partnership for Africa's Development. I believe that this high-level meeting will prove to be an invaluable opportunity for the 189 Member States, both developed and developing, of the United Nations to galvanize their political will in support of NEPAD.

There is a growing awareness that the future of African development will have a profound impact—economically, socially, and politically—on the future of humanity. We all know that in the age of globalization the fate of all the world's peoples is inextricably interlinked with that of the people of

Africa. I would like to call upon all countries, both developed and developing, the private sector, NGOs, and civil society to combine their efforts to bring hope and development to Africa.

When the ideals conceived by the initiators of NEPAD come into reality, both Africans and non-Africans will be able to share a genuine common prosperity and sustainable development.

Toward that goal, we have to work together closely.

Thank you.

vi. Statement at the Meeting of the UN Association of Singapore "The United Nations: What does the world body hold for our future?"

30 August 2002

President Tham, Ladies and Gentlemen:

I am very pleased and honored to address the distinguished members and guests of the UN Association of Singapore. This visit to Singapore is one of my last duties as President of the General Assembly of the United Nations. And I must say that it is much more a pleasure than a duty to come to Singapore and meet with the leaders and intellectuals of this vibrant, beautiful city.

As President of the General Assembly during the past year, I have given much thought to the past, present, and future of the United Nations, made many speeches on the topic, and received valuable feedback from a variety of audiences around the world. And my thoughts have evolved accordingly. It is very gratifying that I should have the chance to discuss the subject with all of you today thanks to the UN Association of Singapore, for I have always found the leaders of this country to be of the highest intellectual and moral caliber.

Indeed, in New York, some of the most articulate and engaging diplomats I have met around the UN have been from Singapore. You can rest assured that you are very well represented at the global body. Meanwhile, here, as I offer you my views on the challenges facing the UN today, and how the world body is trying to meet these challenges and chart its future in these changing times, I expect the ensuing exchange of views with you to be a mutually enriching and thought-inspiring experience.

The world today is certainly a very different place from the world that gave birth to the UN 57 years ago in the aftermath of the Second World War. In designing the new global organization, the founding fathers drew lessons from the unfulfilled idealism of the League of Nations. To make the United Nations viable and enduring, they incorporated many elements of realism into the Charter, especially concerning the composition and decision-making mechanism of the Security Council. Hence, the basic structure of the United Nations was a product of the global political dynamics of that era.

Since then, the world body has evolved with the changing times, with an ever-expanding mandate. Now, hardly anything escapes the attention of the United Nations. If there is an issue, there is bound to be a UN body laboring over the details. How successful has it been? The answer varies. Certainly, few would dispute its accomplishments in areas such as decolonization, peacekeeping, promotion of human rights and democracy, humanitarian assistance, environmental protection, and codification of international law. But still there are those who question the effectiveness of the global organization and even try to discount it as a talking shop, probably out of frustration over seemingly much more discussion than action.

Having presided over the UN meetings for the past year, and being a three-term parliamentarian back home, I, for one, am a staunch advocate of discussion, as well as for the efforts to make it more democratic and result-oriented. Indeed, the United Nations has been engaged in an on-going effort to reform itself toward greater effectiveness and relevance in a world where constant change seems to pervade all aspects of global life. But underneath the fluidity, there are a number of general trends that constitute the dictate of our times and thus the context in which the United Nations is trying to chart its present and future.

First, the field of international relations is becoming increasingly crowded with more and more actors. The expansion of state actors, which has gone from 51 in 1945 to 189 today in terms of UN membership, can be traced back to the decolonization process that culminated in the 1960s. But the increase continues even to this day. Indeed, this year, we will shortly welcome two new members into the fold, Switzerland and East Timor. Furthermore, compared with the initial lot of 51 members, the current membership of the UN comprises a much wider spectrum in political, economic, and cultural background. The dynamics of the world body has dramatically changed accordingly.

Non-state actors have become important players as well. They include collective actors of varying degrees of integra-

141

tion, such as the EU, the African Union, the G-77, the non-aligned Movement, etc. Some of these organizations enjoy observer status in the UN, as do some other political entities such as Palestine or the SWAPO in the past. Furthermore, non-governmental organizations (NGOs) are increasingly recognized by the UN as participants in international life, as sources of input into its deliberations and partners in the implementation of action. It seems evident by now that if the UN aspires toward effective global governance, it must do so with all of these actors fully on board.

Second, the world is no longer ideologically divided by a Cold War, which had been the dominant feature of international relations during the second half of the 20th century. The Cold War set in immediately after the creation of the UN and held the global organization under its grip until it came to an end with the disintegration of the Soviet Union in 1991. Since then, the world has seen fewer and fewer conflicts stemming from ideological rivalry or bloc-to-bloc confrontation, and thus the possibility of global nuclear war has been largely diminished. At the same time, however, conflicts of ethnic or religious origin have proliferated and intensified, drawing the urgent attention of the United Nations. Some, like the Middle East, continue to simmer and remain on the agenda of the world body.

In the post–Cold War era, the United Nations has come to play an expanding role in restoring and maintaining peace. Once introduced to fill in the gap between the idea of collective security and the reality of a lack in Charter provisions for its implementation, the institution of UN peacekeeping operations has evolved into a highly effective means of furthering peace around the world. The world body's peacekeeping capability has been strengthened in recent years with an overhaul of its operations as a whole.

No longer tied down by the ideological rivalry of superpowers, the United Nations is also recharged in its work of bringing the community of nations together in the pursuit of universal values and shared standards, brought under the broad rubric of democracy and market economy. The work is greatly facilitated but also made much more complicated by the third and perhaps the most defining trend of our times, i.e. globalization, which is transforming the world into a virtually single global village.

Globalization has been underway for decades, long before the word became fashionable in public discourse. But the wide use of the term in the final decade of the last century and henceforth is a reflection of its predominance over all aspects of life in the present era.

The recent surge in globalization has been made possible by the revolutionary advances in communication and transportation technology, which have rendered national boundaries increasingly irrelevant for economic, financial, cultural, and even criminal purposes. The interdependence that globalization generates has been most visible in the economic sphere, where the global trade volume has grown 50-fold during the past 50 years, and the cost of a phone call from New York to London reduced to half of one percent of what it used to be in 1950.

Globalization has had far-reaching implications for the work of the United Nations. As states become more interdependent, as problems become more transborder and global, the issues brought to the UN have continued to expand and diversify. Environmental protection has been such an issue, long on the UN's agenda. It is receiving renewed attention as the World Summit on Sustainable Development has just opened in Johannesburg, South Africa, this week.

Furthermore, globalization itself is an issue that the world body must come to terms with. Globalization is proving to be a double-edged sword. While enhancing the well-being of humankind in general, it is also widening the gap between the haves and have-nots within and between countries in the shrinking, global village. The problem is aggravated by the digital divide and other development issues of the information age. In the process, the already vulnerable sectors of society, such as children, the aged, and the disabled, are likely to fall further behind. Bridging the gap, making globalization work to the benefit of all, is one important challenge that the United Nations is called upon to rise up to.

The terrorist attacks of 11 September 2001 and the ensuing events in the international community are illustrative of the three trends and the challenges they pose for the world body. The attacks represent a new type of conflict of the post–Cold War era. They were committed by a transnational terrorist organization, which was able to exploit the cross-border flow of money and information. They have alerted the world to the fact that a terrorist organization, a non-state entity, can pose such a serious threat to international security.

Everyone must remember what happened on 11 September 2001. For me, it was the day of my scheduled inauguration as the President of the General Assembly, which had to be postponed to the next day. The three months since then were marked by the most extraordinary and busiest session in the annals of the General Assembly. During this period, the Assembly had to reorganize virtually all of its work program. One whole week of the Plenary was promptly set aside to debate measures to combat terrorism, during which the Mayor of New York City was invited to speak for the first time at the UN. The fight against terrorism also topped the agenda of the General Debate, rescheduled to November.

A question I am often asked is whether 11 September had the effect of weakening the role of the UN, by diverting attention away to processes taking place elsewhere, more specifically whether the UN's role in the fight against terrorism has been overshadowed by the multinational forces created outside the UN. If one were to focus just on the military campaign in Afghanistan, it might look that way. Certainly, the military campaign was important, but in and around the UN, measures of more fundamental and long-term nature have been considered and taken so as to root out terrorism and to assist the Afghan people in rebuilding their country.

Against terrorism, the UN took a series of actions. In a united voice, the Member States condemned the terrorist attacks in a speedy and firm manner both in the General Assembly and the Security Council. We agreed to measures to suppress the financing of terrorist organizations and endorsed the deployment of the International Security Assistance Force in Afghanistan. We also increased humanitarian assistance for the Afghan people and set up the UN Assistance Mission in Afghanistan (UNAMA), to facilitate recovery there. At the same time, progress has been made in the negotiations to draft a comprehensive convention against terrorism. In sum, multilateral cooperation centering around the UN has gained renewed importance in the global community's efforts to cope with the crisis and to establish measures to stem the growth of terrorism.

Furthermore, 11 September and the ensuing developments in Afghanistan have given added impetus to the deliberations taking place at the UN to redefine the concept of security. During the recent years, concepts such as "new security" and "human security" have come into wide circulation, broadening the debate on security beyond the traditional military and political concerns. The new approach to security issues has been vindicated in the aftermath of 11 September. It has become clear that security cannot be maintained by military means alone. Security, and peace, in this interconnected world of instantaneous communication and blurred boundaries, must be seen as a holistic concept. At the UN, this has meant that security concerns have come to penetrate into all the deliberations. Now, in addition to the Security Council, the General Assembly, the Economic and Social Council, and many other bodies are incorporating security concerns into their own work.

For reasons just discussed, these are challenging times for the UN. The world body may not have fulfilled all of the mandates envisioned by its founding fathers 57 years ago. But it has proven to be resilient and evolving, continually adapting itself to meet new challenges. The UN peacekeeping operations have been a good example.

In April this year, I had an opportunity to see for myself the largest and perhaps most successful UN peacekeeping operation, namely UNAMSIL in Sierra Leone. The following month,

I had the chance to see another UN "success story" in East Timor, where I welcome that country to the family of independent nations on behalf of the General Assembly. Sierra Leone and East Timor are excellent examples of how the UN is responding to the needs and demands of the rapidly changing world.

Also underway at the UN are efforts to better adapt itself to the new international conditions. Deliberations are underway on the reform of the Security Council as well as on the revitalization of the General Assembly. The outcome of these deliberations concerning the two vital organs of the United Nations will have far-reaching implications for the future of the organization.

As a means to revitalize the General Assembly, a small but important change has been made. The rules of procedure of the General Assembly have been amended to elect the President and other officials at least three months in advance, so as to give them time to prepare and provide continuity to the work of the GA President. Thus, on 8 July, Deputy Prime Minister Jan Kavan of the Czech Republic was elected as my successor, as were the 21 GA Vice-Presidents and the Chairpersons of the six Main Committees of the 57th Session of the Assembly. The transition from my presidency to Mr. Kavan's will set a precedent for future sessions of the General Assembly as well as for other bodies in the UN system.

Finally, a few words on the relations between the United Nations and regional cooperation. We all know that Singapore is a leading force in regional cooperation in this part of the world, as has been the case with APEC or ASEM. Regional cooperation of varying degrees of integration has been on the rise, particularly during the last decade. At the current stage, most of these bodies of regional cooperation, with a few exceptions including the European Union, are concentrating on economic issues with a much lower degree of institutionalization compared to those in the UN system. Thus, the linkage between the UN and regional cooperation is not very strong for now. However, like we have witnessed in the EU, regional cooperation is an evolving process. And as regional cooperation in East Asia develops into a deeper and more comprehensive stage, I believe there will be wider and closer cooperation with the UN and other international organizations. After all, many of their goals are shared and approaches are complementary. This is certainly an important area to be explored for the future of the UN and states of every region in the world.

I have tried to look at how the UN is adapting and reforming itself to meet new challenges at this changing, critical time. For the longer term, we must ask ourselves how we see the world's only global organization developing in the coming decades. Would it develop into a kind of world government, or would it remain a forum for nation-states? The answers do not come easy and would depend on fundamental, philosophical questions about the nature of history, human societies, and nation-states.

In any case, being the optimist that I am, I believe that we must begin to explore those questions by placing greater hope in the UN. We seek greater safety and well-being for humanity in general, and for this we need greater predictability and rule of law in international life. We should make the interaction among the ever-growing number of actors in the globalized world more peaceful than violent, more cooperative than confrontational, more productive than wasteful. And at the center of all of these efforts, we need the United Nations, the only universal body, doing more than less in its endeavor to fulfill its mission of strengthening peace and human well-being around the world. Thank you.

9 September 2002

Excellencies, Mr. Secretary-General, Distinguished Delegates, Ladies and Gentlemen:

We have now come to the end of the 56th Session of the General Assembly, and it is time for me to declare the Session closed. Looking back over the past year, I am sure we are all overwhelmed and humbled by a flood of thoughts and emotions. Words such as "extraordinary," "unusual," or "unprecedented" have been used to characterize our Session, so much so that they have become cliché by now. I have been deeply honored and privileged to serve as President of the General Assembly during this unique and eventful year of great accomplishments for the United Nations. Allow me to share with you some of my thoughts on this occasion.

Our Session began in a state of crisis, triggered by the most atrocious acts of terrorism in history. My term as President was to start on September 11, 2001, a date now etched in everyone's memory for a very different event. Under serious security threats to the UN headquarters building itself, I had urgent consultations with Secretary-General Kofi Annan. We decided to open the General Assembly the next day, on 12 September. Directly after my assumption as President, the General Assembly adopted its first resolution of the Session (resolution 56/1), condemning strongly the terrorist attacks and calling for international cooperation to eradicate terrorism.

149

The three months following that day turned out to be one of the most extraordinary and demanding periods in the annals of the General Assembly. We had to reorganize virtually all of our work programs. We devoted one whole week of our debate to measures to combat terrorism, during which the Mayor of New York City was invited to speak for the first time at the UN. We also held a two-day meeting on the theme "Dialogue among Civilizations" to promote intercultural understanding, which had particular relevance in the context of our pressing concern with terrorism.

Terrorism also topped the agenda of the General Debate, which was held in November, two months later than usual, over a period of only seven days, but still with the participation of 187 delegations, including 41 Heads of State or Government. Joined in the view that international terrorism constitutes a threat to international peace and security as well as a crime against humanity, Member States underscored the key role to be played by the United Nations in intensifying international efforts to eliminate terrorism. Many also cautioned that the fight against terrorism should not be connected with any religion or ethnicity.

The heightened awareness about the nature and threat of terrorism has been paralleled by progress in strengthening the legal framework against terrorism, especially through the work of the Sixth Committee. The Assembly has accelerated its work with a view to an early conclusion of a comprehensive convention on international terrorism. At the same time, I have urged Member States that have not yet done so to become parties, as a matter of priority, to the existing international conventions relating to terrorism. I hope that the momentum we have created will be built upon during the next session so that the remaining questions can be resolved toward the establishment of a more effective legal framework to root out terrorism.

Also high on our agenda has been the question of Afghanistan. The General Assembly has taken coordinated measures with the Security Council to restore peace and security in the war-ravaged nation and to assist in its reconstruction. We welcomed the establishment of the UN Assistance Mission in Afghanistan (UNAMA) and warmly appreciated the efforts of the Secretary-General and his Special Representative to promote peace and security in that county. We have responded promptly and concretely to the needs of the Afghan people, for massive humanitarian assistance as well as support in their post-conflict reconstruction efforts.

Thus coping with the new challenges, we have also been steadfast in furthering important work already begun. Being the first session of the General Assembly after the historic Millennium Assembly of 2000, our meetings made major advances in the follow-up to the Millennium Declaration. Noting with appreciation the road map report of the Secretary-General the Assembly recommended that it be considered a useful guide in the implementation of the Declaration by the UN system and requested the Secretary-General to prepare annual as well as five-year comprehensive reports on progress achieved toward implementing the Declaration.

In this regard, I called upon Member States to sustain the political will of the Millennium Summit and take comprehensive and balanced measures to turn the goals of the Millennium Declaration into reality. The implementation of the Declaration can be effective only through the participation of and cooperation among all actors, including States, the United Nations system, other international and regional organizations, and also civil society.

On the economic front, too, it has been a challenging time for us. With much of the global attention focused on the fight against terrorism and the world economy moving perilously close to another recession, we still managed to make progress in a number of important areas. In particular, we have moved forward in our pursuit of development. There have been major events and actions toward the implementation of the Millennium development goals. In the process, the Assembly has maintained its focus, among others, on the eradication of poverty.

The momentum generated by the Millennium Summit has been preserved through major UN meetings on development held in and outside New York, such as the International Conference on Financing for Development in March, the meeting of the General Assembly devoted to Information and Communication Technologies for Development in June, and the World Summit on Sustainable Development held earlier this month. By addressing the critical issues of development financing, the digital divide, and sustainable development, respectively, these landmark gatherings have made vital contributions to the international community's endeavors to achieve economic and social development objectives.

In this regard, I have accorded particular priority to the issue of development of Africa. African development, a common element that cuts across the issues of poverty eradication, HIV/AIDS, sustainable development, and conflict prevention has become one of the most daunting challenges of our times

It is in this context that last April I visited four West African countries—Ghana, Sierra Leone, The Gambia, and Senegal. During these visits, I reaffirmed the strong support of the UN system for the efforts of the African countries to promote economic and political development and exchanged views with their leaders on finding better ways and means to realize our common goals.

This year, with the final review of the United Nations New Agenda for the Development of Africa in the 1990s (UN-NADAF) underway, we have welcomed the New Partnership for Africa's Development (NEPAD) on which a high-level plenary meeting of the General Assembly will be held next week. Learning from the lessons of UN-NADAF, we have renewed our commitment to promoting African development in all its aspects. In a related development, the Assembly's decision last year to create the Office of the High Representative for the Least Developed Countries, Landlocked Countries and Small Islands Developing States should be considered a major step forward in advocating the cause of all LDCs.

Our achievements have been no less substantial in the area of human rights and social issues. Postponed in the aftermath of September 11, the Special Session on Children held in May this year proved to be a historic gathering of world leaders to reaffirm their commitment toward building a "world fit for children." At the opposite end of the age spectrum, the Second World Assembly on Ageing produced a plan of action that will guide our efforts to meet the challenges of aging populations and their far-reaching socio-economic consequences.

In these and other endeavors of the UN, civil society has become an increasingly important partner. Multi-stakeholder participation has now become established practice in areas as diverse as health and immunization, the rights and well-being of children, and harnessing information and communication technologies for development. I would like to express my satisfaction with the Assembly's growing recognition of the instrumental contributions by NGOs and civil society in general to our work in the economic, social, and other related fields.

Meanwhile, we have taken a big step forward in reforming the United Nations, with a small but significant change. Through a series of informal meetings of the plenary, we were able to amend the relevant Rules of Procedure of the General Assembly to elect the President and other officials at least three months before the beginning of a new session. This change does not merely represent a procedural modification. It is designed to ensure a more efficient transition and continuity between successive presidencies and thus facilitate and strengthen the role of the President.

In accordance with the new rules, former Deputy Prime Minister and Minister of Foreign Affairs Jan Kavan of the Czech Republic was elected as my successor, as were the 21 vice-presidents and the six Main Committee chairmen for the 57th Session of the Assembly. Since then, I have met with President-elect Kavan, as have our two cabinet teams, in many consultations to cover all issues relating to our transition. Indeed, this has been the first substantive transition process for the presidency, and it should set a precedent for future sessions of the General Assembly and other bodies in the UN system.

We have also deliberated the issue of Security Council reform through the Open-Ended Working Group, which met in four sessions from February to July this year. Now in its ninth year, the Working Group has made some progress in the area of the working methods of the Security Council. The more difficult area of membership expansion has not seen much change except for the addition of a few new proposals. More active debate is expected during the tenth year of the Working Group.

On a day-to-day level, I have endeavored to improve the way we conduct the business of the General Assembly. To make our meetings most efficient, especially when they had to be shortened and condensed due to the contingencies of last year, I called for punctuality with time and parsimony with words on the part of everyone. I kept my door open all the time and met with as many people as I could. I also consulted as often as possible with the Presidents of the Security Council and ECOSOC as well as the Chairmen of Regional Groups.

As we look back on the 56th Session, the magnitude and intensity of our work are reflected in the numbers. We have dealt with 173 agenda items, held 112 plenary meetings, and adopted 359 resolutions and 107 decisions. We also held a special session and three rounds of a resumed emergency special session, where altogether five resolutions and nine decisions were adopted.

As President of the General Assembly, I paid official visits to 12 countries. They are, in the order of my visits, Ghana, Sierra Leone, The Gambia, Senegal, East Timor on its independence, Japan, Italy, the Holy See, Austria, the Czech Republic, Australia, and Singapore, I wish to take this opportunity to thank their respective governments once again for their cooperation and hospitality. I also visited the UN offices in Geneva and Vienna, as well as the UN peacekeepers at UN-AMSIL in Sierra Leone.

Thus reviewing the past one year, I would not be fair if I did not mention the tasks that remain unfinished and need to be dealt with continuously by my successors. These include, among others, measures to eliminate terrorism, conflict prevention, Security Council reform, and revitalization of the General Assembly. With regard to the last item in particular, I believe that greater consideration should be given to ways to strengthen and institutionalize the role of the President of the General Assembly, not only in terms of the General Assembly but also with regard to UN meetings held away from the headquarters. We must also heed the views of some Member States that the recent surge of mega conferences held outside the UN bodies proper could end up marginalizing the latter and thus run counter to our goal of strengthening and revitalizing the role of major UN organs.

Distinguished Delegates and Colleagues,

The world today is certainly a very different place from the world that gave birth to the United Nations 57 years ago in the aftermath of the Second World War. There have been so many changes, of which I would like to mention three that directly relate to the future of our world body.

First, the field of international relations is becoming increasingly crowded with more and more actors. The UN membership has grown from 51 in 1945 to 189 today. The increase continues even to this day, as we will shortly welcome two new members, Switzerland and East Timor. Furthermore, compared with the initial lot of 51 members, the current membership of the UN comprises a much wider spectrum in political, economic, and cultural backgrounds. The dynamics of the world body has dramatically changed accordingly. At the same time, non-state actors have become important players as well, such as international or regional organizations and non-governmental organizations.

Second, the world is no longer ideologically divided by a Cold War, which had been the dominant feature of international relations during the second half of the 20th century. In the post–Cold War era, the United Nations has come to play an expanding role in restoring and maintaining peace. Once introduced to fill in the gap between the idea of collective security and the reality of unimplemented Charter provisions, UN peacekeeping operations have evolved into a highly effective means of furthering peace around the world. At the same time, our world body is recharged in its work of bringing the community of nations together in the pursuit of universal values and shared standards, brought under the broad rubric of democracy and market economy.

Third, globalization has come to affect every aspect of international life with far-reaching implications for the work of the United Nations. As states become more interdependent, as problems become more transborder and global, the issues brought to the UN have continued to expand and diversify. In the process, we find ourselves dealing both with positive and negative aspects of globalization. While enhancing the well-being of humankind in general, globalization also widens the gap between the haves and have-nots within and between countries. Bridging the gap, making globalization work to the benefit of all, is one important challenge that the United Nations must rise up to.

The future of the United Nations depends on how the world body adapts and reforms itself to meet the new challenges in the changing world.

In the final weeks of our work of the main part of our Session last December, we were all delighted and heartened by the awarding of the Nobel Peace Prize jointly to the United Nations and Secretary-General Kofi Annan. A number of UN agencies had received the prize before, but this was the first time that the United Nations as a whole was so honored. As I stated at that time, the prize should be viewed as both recognition of past achievements as well as a summons to move forward toward our goals with renewed energy and dedication. It represents the expectations of the peoples of the world for the United Nations to stand equal to the new challenges facing humankind.

We should not be complacent either about the UN's achievements or its future roles. To be sure, the organization has its shortcoming. UN initiatives have not always been successful, nor have its successes always been permanent. Criticism of the United Nations, both fair and unfair, has been a staple of political debate since 1945. Some of the more constructive criticisms have served as useful bases for exploring ways to improve the work of the organization.

For the longer term, we must ask ourselves how we see the world's only global organization developing in the coming decades. Would it develop into a kind of world government, or would it remain a forum for nation-states? The answers do not come easily and would depend on fundamental, philosophical questions about the nature of history, human societies, and nation-states.

In any case, being the optimist that I am, I believe that we must begin to explore these questions by placing greater hope in the UN. If we seek greater safety and well-being for

158

humanity in general, there must be greater predictability and rule of law in international life. In this rapidly globalizing world, more numerous and diverse actors interact with one another on a constant basis. We should make these interactions more peaceful than violent, more cooperative than confrontational, more productive than wasteful. And at the center of all of these efforts, we need the United Nations, the only universal body, doing more than less.

Excellencies, Ladies and Gentlemen,

Now, I believe it is time for me to express my deepest appreciation to all who have helped and supported me in discharging my duties.

First of all, my sincere gratitude goes to all delegates of Member States for their active participation in the meetings and their guidance in conducting the business of the General Assembly. Then I wish to thank the Vice-Presidents, who have kindly taken my place on many occasions, and the Chairmen, Vice-Chairmen, and Rapporteurs of the Main Committees, who did excellent work despite numerous difficulties under unusual circumstances. I should also like to thank the Vice-Chairpersons of the Open-Ended Working Group on Security Council reform and all those distinguished diplomats who worked with me as facilitators on several important issues, including revitalization of the General Assembly and conflict prevention.

My heartfelt appreciation goes to Secretary-General Kofi Annan, for his invaluable support and guidance. Under-Secretary-General Chen Jian and his dedicated staff of the Department for General Assembly Affairs and Conference

Services, whose name will be changed to the Department for General Assembly and Conference Management, as well as my own office staff have consistently provided top-quality, professional assistance. I am immensely grateful to them and all other members of the Secretariat, including the security officers and interpreters. Last but not least, I thank the government and people of my home country, the Republic of Korea. Whether as Foreign Minister or a former Minister, I have always enjoyed their unwavering support for the success of this presidency. Needless to say, there are many others not mentioned here, but to whom I am equally indebted.

Finally, I would like to offer my best wishes to my successor, President Jan Kavan. I am confident that under his able stewardship, the 57th Session of the General Assembly will see most fruitful results.

Thank you.

Appendix II: Major Events During President Han Seung-soo's Term in Office

September 2001 to August 2002

Sep. 10   The United Nations Security Council unan imously adopts a resolution to lift the arms embargo on Yugoslavia, thereby lifting all UN sanctions against Yugoslavia

Sep. 11   Multiple terrorist attacks on the United States

Sep. 12   The 56th session of the UN General Assembly begins, and South Korean Minister of Foreign Affairs and Trade Han Seung-soo is appointed president of the General Assembly

Oct. 3   UN Secretary-General Kofi Annan appoints Lakhdar Brahimi, former minister for for- eign affairs of Algeria, as special representa- tive of the secretary-general for Afghanistan

Oct. 7   Britain and the United States begin aerial bombings of military facilities of the Taliban government and al-Qaeda facilities in retali- ation for the September 11 terrorist attacks on the United States and begin aerial deliv- ery of food and other humanitarian relief supplies in Afghanistan

Oct. 12	The Norwegian Nobel Committee announces its decision to award the Nobel Peace Prize for the centennial year of 2001 to the United Nations and Secretary-General Annan in recognition of their response to "such new challenges as HIV/AIDS and international terrorism"
Nov. 1	UN Secretary-General Annan states that US bombings on Afghanistan are an "impediment" to humanitarian relief activities by the United Nations at a press conference in Geneva, Switzerland, and requests an early end to the bombings
Nov. 4	The 10 members of the Association of Southeast Asian Nations adopt the Declaration on Joint Action to Counter Terrorism, expressing their determination to strengthen efforts to eradicate terrorism, in Bandar Seri Begawan, Brunei Darussalam
Nov. 4	Anthrax attacks in the United States
Nov. 5	The First Committee (Disarmament and International Security) of the UN General Assembly adopts a nuclear disarmament resolution proposed by Japan with 124 votes for and two against
Nov. 13	At a UN Security Council meeting, Special Representative Brahimi proposes an initiative to form an interim council comprising

representatives of all Afghan ethnic groups and regions toward the establishment of a new Afghan government for the first time in two years

Nov. 14   The World Trade Organization Ministerial Conference, having commenced on November 9 in Doha, Qatar, and having approved China's accession to the WTO on November 10 and Taiwan's accession on November 11, concludes after adopting the Doha Development Agenda, a ministerial declaration stipulating the start of a new round of multilateral trade negotiations in several areas, including the review of agricultural, antidumping, and other rules

Dec. 3   The ministerial-level meeting of the Tokyo International Conference on African Development to discuss economic development in African countries and assistance by developed nations is held in Tokyo

Dec. 5   Four Afghan factions, including the Northern Alliance and the monarchists, agree on the UN proposal for an interim government at negotiations on the establishment of an interim government and sign the Interim Afghan Government Agreement

Dec. 6   The Afghan Women's Summit, which began on December 4 in Brussels, Belgium, adopts a declaration calling for equal rights for women in all areas and the expansion of women's education rights

Dec. 7   The Biological and Toxin Weapons Convention Review Conference held in Geneva is cut short without adopting a final statement due to divisions between the United States and other countries over major issues

Dec. 11   The European Council announces the continuation of monetary assistance to the Korean Peninsula Energy Development Organization until 2005

Dec. 13   US President George W. Bush announces that he has notified the Russian government of the United States' unilateral withdrawal from the Anti-Ballistic Missile Treaty, which it signed with the Soviet Union in 1972; Russian President Vladimir Putin criticizes the move as a "mistake" and propose the creation of a new security framework

Dec. 20   At an emergency session, the UN General Assembly adopts a resolution to set up a UN-led monitoring mechanism in the region to prevent the expansion of hostilities between Israel and the Palestinian Authority

The UN Security Council unanimously adopts a resolution to dispatch multina-

164

	tional forces of between 3,000 and 5,000 troops led by Britain to the Afghan capital of Kabul
Dec. 22	The interim Afghan administration is inaugurated, and Hamid Karzai, an influential figure of the Pashtuns, the largest ethnic group in Afghanistan, takes office as chair (prime minister)
Jan. 4, 2002	In Kabul, in the presence of Special Representative Brahimi, the interim Afghan administration and the International Security Assistance Force sign an agreement on military deployment
Jan. 21	The International Conference on Reconstruction Assistance to Afghanistan is held in Tokyo with the attendance of 83 countries and international organizations, and a Co-Chairs' Summary of Conclusions is issued stipulating monetary assistance totaling ¥600 billion, the establishment of a trust fund in the World Bank, and the placement of an Implementation Group in Kabul
Jan. 28	The WTO holds the first meeting of the Trade Negotiations Committee in Geneva, marking the full-fledged start of the new round of multilateral trade negotiations
Jan. 29	US President Bush gives his first State of the Union address, in which he labels North

Korea, Iran, and Iraq as an "axis of evil" that aims to threaten the United States and its allies by developing or obtaining weapons of mass destruction and declares that the United States will continue its war on terror throughout the world

Feb. 1   US President Bush announces his intention to engage in talks with North Korea if the latter reduces its conventional weapons deployed around the demilitarized zone

US Secretary of State Colin Powell meets with South Korean Minister of Foreign Affairs and Trade Han Seung-soo and reaffirms that President Bush's criticism of North Korea and two other countries as constituting an "axis of evil" does not signify a change in US policy toward North Korea and that the United States continues to support South Korea's sunshine policy

Feb. 25   A United Nations spokesperson announces that Secretary-General Annan and Iraqi Minister of Foreign Affairs Naji Sabri met in New York in March, resuming dialogue between the United Nations and Iraq, which had been stalled since March 2001 due to tensions over UN inspections for weapons of mass destruction

Mar. 21   The summit-level meeting of the UN International Conference on Financing for

Development begins in Monterrey, Mexico, to discuss the procurement of funds for the sustainable development of developing countries, and Secretary-General Annan requests developed countries to double their official development assistance

Apr. 19   The G7 Meeting of Financial Ministers and Central Bank Governors begins in Washington, D.C., and a joint statement is adopted noting that the global economy has overcome the effects of the September 2001 terrorist attacks on the United States and is back on a recovery track

May 8   The Special Session of the UN General Assembly on Children begins

May 20   East Timor, which had been under interim UN administration after a quarter century of Indonesian annexation and rule, reaches independence, and the new state of the Democratic Republic of Timor-Leste is born

May 24   US President Bush and Russian President Putin meet and sign the Strategic Offensive Reductions Treaty, which stipulates the reduction of both nations' strategic nuclear warheads by 2012 to one-third of current levels, or 1,700 and 2,200, respectively

May 31   The first soccer World Cup in Asia, cohosted by Japan and South Korea, kicks off in Seoul

Jun. 18	The UN Conference on Trade and Development releases the 2002 Least Developed Countries Report, in which it warns that by 2015 the worldwide number of absolute poor, who live on $1 or less per day, may increase by 37 percent from the current 370 million to 420 million
Jul. 1	The Rome Statute of the International Criminal Court takes effect, and the ICC, which prosecutes individuals accused of genocide and war crimes, is established as the world's first permanent court for prosecuting war crimes
Aug. 5	The UN General Assembly adopts a resolution calling on Israel to withdraw its troops from the Palestinian territories
Aug. 26	The UN World Summit on Sustainable Development (Environment and Development Summit) begins

Index

Perfiliev, Vadim, 10

P5, 103

Plenary meeting, on measures to eliminate international terrorism, 45–47

Powell, Colin, 24, 41

    at Constructing Solidarity for a Stable World, 107

    Han Seung-soo meeting with, on axis of evil talk, 167

    joint press conference with, 56

    post 9/11 initial meeting with, 56

    talks with South Korea of, 167

President of United Nations

    acceptance speech as, 12 September 2001, 113–119

    countries of origin of, 100

    election of, 9/11 events on, 7–8, 11–17

    enhancing efficiency of, 105–106

    Foreign Ministers as, 104

    inauguration as, 8–11

    office location of, 11–12

    other posts held by, 99–100

    qualifications for, 103–104

    reasons for acceptance of, 15–17

    recent history of, 18

    representative role of, 99

    selection of, by regional groups, 99–101

    transition period for, 105–107

President of United Nations, Office of, 75–98

    budget of, 75

    protocol war of nerves with Secretary-General's office of, 77–79

    size and functions of, 75–77

Prime Ministers. *See also specific individuals*

protocol for, 38

Prodi, Romano, 88

Protocol

    for heads of state and dignitaries, 37–39

    order of speakers at UN in, 34–39

182